SCHOLASTIC

35 Independent Math Learning Centers

by Deborah Allen Wirth

NEW YORK • TORONTO • LONDON • AUCKLAND • SYDNEY
MEXICO CITY • NEW DELHI • HONG KONG • BUENOS AIRES

Teaching Resources

Dedication

To Bill, Chelsey, and Mitch—
the loves in my life.

Acknowledgments

Hugs and kisses go to my husband, Bill, and my two children, Chelsey and Mitch. There have been countless hours that they have accompanied me to school after hours, during a holiday, or on weekends, as I worked to enhance classroom activities or practices. More importantly, it has been through watching my own children's experiences that I have grown to become a better teacher. Our strength together as a family has given me the strength I need in all areas of my life.

I am also grateful to Dover Area School District of Pennsylvania, its community, my colleagues and administrators, parents, and especially students who have supported my efforts and given me inspiration along the way. Additionally, I would like to thank Shippensburg University and its staff for providing invaluable professional development activities and opportunities.

Finally, I am forever indebted to my parents, my brother, and my sisters for contributing to the foundation I needed to follow all my dreams. Their continued support and encouragement have helped me tremendously in both professional and personal endeavors.

Cover design by Jim Sarfati
Cover photos by Deborah Allen Wirth; Bonnie Kamin/Photo Edit
Interior design by Sydney Wright; Interior illustrations by Maxie Chambliss and Lillian Kohli

ISBN 0-439-51777-X

Contents

* Assessment sheets provided

Introduction

After teaching second grade for many years, I was very excited when I had the opportunity to change grade levels and become a first-grade teacher. As expected, I had the range of readers—nonreaders, below-grade-level readers, on-grade-level readers, and above-grade-level readers. Since I had successfully learned how to differentiate my reading instruction through the use of guided reading, I was confident the guided reading process would serve the children well. I used an assessment tool to determine the reading level of my students and then incorporated small group instruction to better meet the needs of these readers at their instructional level. Literacy centers were a key component because they provided practice opportunities with various standards. When students used the centers, I was able to find the time to meet with small groups.

However, I was concerned about the range of content knowledge that these same students had in math. For example, through daily calendar activities, I was able to informally determine that a nonreader knew multiplication concepts, an on-grade-level reader could count a large collection of coins, and yet an above-grade-level reader struggled with identification of two-digit numerals. Up to this point, most of my math instruction tended to be whole group with little focus on differentiation. Now I realized the need to change my approach to math instruction. Because I had already implemented guided reading to meet these students' individual instructional needs in language arts, it occurred to me that I could adapt this strategy in the area of mathematics.

What Is Guided Math?

As the name suggests, guided math is a strategy paralleling guided reading. Both guided math and guided reading are strategies that differentiate instruction to better meet the needs of all learners. During my guided math block, I have shifted the focus away from whole group instruction. I now spend the majority of time on small group instruction and practice opportunities—both essential for success. Whole group instruction still occurs, but in a much smaller chunk of time, serving as the springboard (or foundation) for the small group instruction and independent practice that follows.

A major difference between guided math and guided reading is the type of assessment necessary to determine the learners' needs. In guided reading, there are many types of assessments for determining reading levels. Your district probably has embraced a particular type. Generally speaking, once a reading level is determined, the growth of a child's reading ability is somewhat predictable (of course, there are always exceptions!). Groups formed during guided reading are usually based upon a child's reading level.

The assessment process is not as definitive for guided math. For example, a child may be very proficient in the area of number and operations but still lack the geometric concepts that are typical for that age level. Another may be able to use standard measurement yet lack algebraic patterning skills. Although a beginning-of-the-year math inventory provides an overriding sense of a child's math ability, it is not the most effective tool. Instead, individual pretests addressing particular units or content are more effective. Therefore, groups formed during guided math are usually based upon a child's content knowledge in a particular unit of study.

Guided Math Components	Balanced Reading Components
Whole group instruction	Shared reading
Individualized or small group instruction	Guided reading
Independent practice	Independent reading
Math activities/centers	Literacy activities/centers

Many of my guided math components are similar to those found in my balanced reading program.

Regardless of the assessment used, the purpose is clear: Teachers first must determine the needs of the students. This, in turn, determines the type of small group instruction that will occur. The flow of children in and out of groups based upon their needs is what we refer to as flexible grouping. It may be obvious, then, that your flexible grouping within the guided math framework is usually much more fluid than that of guided reading.

I have found that a natural transition for my guided math approach occurs once students learn the guided reading procedures necessary for independent and small-group learning and practice.

Pretesting: An Essential in Guided Math

Pretesting is a crucial step in the guided math process. It helps to determine what your students do or do not know in a particular content strand of math. As mentioned earlier, this information is essential in order to place students in the most effective instructional grouping situation. The best way to do this is by administering a pretest for each upcoming unit. If you have a textbook series, pretests may already be available to you as part of the resource package. If not, an alternate form of a chapter test may serve as a pretest. Otherwise, you will need to develop one yourself based on the unit you are about to teach. Despite the time and effort it takes to make your own pretesting tool, the time you save in the long run is invaluable.

How to Begin

As you can imagine, it is very important to explain the purpose of a pretest to students. Without doing so, they may become overwhelmed and stressed. In child-friendly language, let students know that the pretest will drive your instruction.

Administration

A few days before you begin a math unit, give the pretest to students. Explain that if they are unable to complete a problem, they should put a question mark by the problem rather than leave it blank. That way, you are assured that they saw the problem and did not skip it accidentally.

Correcting the Pretest

Using a highlighter, circle incorrect answers and question marks. Do not fill in the correct answers for them and do not put a score on the pretest (you will hand it back to students toward the end of the unit so that students may correct their mistakes).

Compiling the Information

On your own copy of the pretest in the top right hand corner, list the names of any students who got the entire pretest correct. Next to each test question, list the name of any student who got the respective question wrong or did not answer the question. In essence, you are doing an item analysis of the test.

Using the Information to Drive Instruction

Taking the compiled information from the pretest, you may want to make notes in your teacher or curriculum manual. For example, on the pretest it may become evident that three of your students are struggling with coin identification. List their names on the respective lesson that addresses this concept. It will prompt you to pay careful attention to them during your whole group mini-lesson. You may even want to prepare reteaching worksheets for them to use in the event they struggle during the mini-lesson. On the flip side, you can prepare enrichment activities for those children who passed the entire pretest.

Returning the Pretest

As the unit comes to an end, return the original unit pretest to students. Again, this is not for use as a test grade, but rather as a record of the child's growth in the content over time. Have students make their corrections using a colored pencil. This makes the record of growth more evident while illustrating to students and their parents the original mistakes. Moreover, the correction process gives you one more chance to reteach in order to prepare the child for the summative evaluation of the unit. This pretest may also serve as a study guide to use at home as students prepare for the end-of-unit assessment.

An Important Note Regarding Pretests

One cannot automatically assume that if a child correctly answers a question that she or he truly understands the content. Perhaps the child had a lucky guess. Or, if a child answers a question incorrectly, it is quite possible that the child may understand the concept once she or he participates in the whole group mini-lesson and guided practice. The pretest, then, serves as a guide in planning instruction. Constant monitoring and informal assessment is a must as the unit progresses.

Guided Math Components

Whole Group Instruction

In guided math, whole group instruction is similar to a mini-lesson lasting 10 to 20 minutes. It is a brief, hands-on activity that teaches children the overriding concept of a particular lesson. Afterwards, a "guided practice" opportunity occurs. In my classroom, this often is a brief workbook exercise that takes children from a concrete to a more abstract model of a particular concept. This guided practice activity is also done as a whole group activity.

Small Group Instruction

The mini-lesson from the whole group instruction becomes the springboard (or foundation) for learners during this component of guided math. For example, an exciting new concept for most second graders is learning how to add two-digit numbers with regrouping. Our whole group instruction activity uses base ten blocks to demonstrate the regrouping process of the ones' place. During guided practice, students record the regrouped ones on a workbook page. During small group instruction, this same process is used to show regrouping of tens or even hundreds for those students who have already demonstrated mastery of this second-grade objective. For those who still have difficulty with basic addition, a trading game using ones and tens blocks helps to reinforce the regrouping concept.

◆ I keep my eyes and ears open for "outdated" computers that no one wants anymore (I have three such computers in my classroom!). The software I use is usually district-owned.

◆ Yard sales are terrific places to find low-priced computer software, as well as many classroom games that reinforce math concepts and problem-solving skills.

Independent Practice

This occurs concurrently with small group instruction after the brief whole group instruction and guided practice. Students complete a short independent activity, workbook page, or worksheet to demonstrate their understanding of the taught concept. Depending on the pretest results or what you may have observed during the mini-lesson, some children may need an enrichment or reteaching activity instead. Recognizing the need for more differentiated activities, most publishers of recent math textbook series provide reteaching, practice, and enrichment resource books as a component of their series. If you do not have these, you may need to develop practice sheets that will address the range of ability levels.

Using the previous regrouping illustration, children who can already regroup ones will complete an enrichment sheet that accompanies that particular lesson rather than complete the corresponding workbook page. Or, if such a sheet is not readily available, students can copy on a sheet of paper four appropriate problems that involve regrouping in the tens place. (Remember, as part of your guided math time, you will meet with these children in a small group setting. Therefore, the independent practice can be an outgrowth of your small group instruction.)

Conversely, you may give a reteaching sheet to students still struggling with the concept. Or you can choose a practice activity based on the small group instruction. You might invite students to demonstrate their practice within your small group setting instead. For example, ask this group to add two one-digit numerals and represent the answer as a ten and ones using base ten blocks.

When enrichment and/or re-teaching is necessary *before* assigning the respective practice activity, other students will need to begin center activities until they meet with you.

Center Activities

The bulk of this book is devoted to center activities that reinforce the NCTM standards. As part of the guided math process, however, it is necessary to redefine the purpose of these centers. First and foremost, these centers provide practice opportunities not only with the current content being taught, but also with previous content. Years back, if I were teaching a unit on money, all of the centers would have included activities reinforcing money. Current brain-based research illustrates that children need many practice opportunities in order to keep content fresh. The cliché "use it or lose it" comes to mind. One of the key benefits I have seen with my guided math approach is what I refer to as "mastery maintenance." Months after I have taught a unit on money, my students are able to retain their knowledge of money due to repeated practice opportunities they have during the center component of my guided math block. Secondly, center activities give you the time needed to conduct small group or individual instruction. Further discussion of centers and how to manage them comes later during this introduction.

Scheduling

I have found that having at least a one-hour block for guided math per day is most effective. If I have less time due to special classes, assemblies, or weather delays, I make some minor adaptations to my guided math block. If you find that you are unable to schedule such a block, you can change the number of guided math components or centers to accommodate your students' needs.

Mrs. Wirth's Schedule

	DAY A	DAY B	DAY C	DAY D	DAY E	DAY F
7:55–8:25	Opening/Journal	Opening/Journal	Opening/Journal	Opening/Journal	Opening/Journal	Opening/Journal
8:25–8:45	Morning Meeting	Morning Meeting	Morning Meeting	Morning Meeting	Morning Meeting	Morning Meeting
8:45–9:50	Math	Math 8:45–9:25 / Library 9:25–10:00	Math	Math	Math	Math
9:50–10:00	Recess	Recess 10:05–10:15	Recess	Recess	Recess	Recess
10:00–10:20	Read Aloud	Secret Message	Read Aloud	Read Aloud	Read Aloud	Art 10:05–10:50
10:20–11:35	P.E. 10:20–10:55 / Shared Reading 10:55–11:35	Spelling/Cursive / Shared Reading	Spelling/Cursive / Shared Reading	Music 10:25–11:00 / Shared Reading 11:00–11:35	Spelling/Cursive / Shared Reading	Shared Reading 10:50–11:35
11:35–12:10	Lunch	Lunch	Lunch	Lunch	Lunch	Lunch
12:15–12:45	Computer Lab	Computer Lab	Computer Lab	Spelling/Cursive	Computer Lab	Spelling/Cursive
12:45–1:15	Science/SS/Health	Science/SS/Health	Science/SS/Health	Science/SS/Health	Science/SS/Health	Science/SS/Health
1:15–2:00	Guided Reading	Guided Reading	Guided Reading	Guided Reading	Guided Reading	Guided Reading
2:00–2:10	Cleanup/Jobs	Cleanup/Jobs	Cleanup/Jobs	Cleanup/Jobs	Cleanup/Jobs	Cleanup/Jobs
2:10–2:20	Time Line/Novel	Time Line/Novel	Time Line/Novel	Time Line/Novel	Time Line/Novel	Time Line/Novel

Here is a sample break down of my guided math block. The times listed are an approximate value and may change depending on the nature of the concepts being taught. More important, you should notice that many activities run concurrently.

Mrs. Wirth's Math Schedule

Time	Activity	Setting	Teacher's Role	Students' Role
8:45–9:05	Guided practice	Whole group	Teach a mini-lesson on a particular concept.	Participate in activity.
9:05–9:45	Independent practice	Individualized	Provide a worksheet or workbook page relating to the concept being taught.	Complete worksheet or workbook page.
	Guided math instruction	Small group or individualized instruction	Work with ability groups based upon known or unknown content.	Meet with teacher when called.
	Center activities	Color groups or individualized	Periodically scan classroom to be sure students are on task and appropriately interacting with centers.	Quietly complete centers according to color group assignment.
9:45–9:50	Wrap-up session	Whole group	Review problem of the day answer and collect any worksheets/workbook pages.	Participate in problem of the day solution. Turn in any completed sheets requested by teacher.

Teaching a Math Unit: Guided Math in Action

❑ Identify upcoming math unit. .... | Money |

❑ Determine whole group mini-lessons (the individual lessons within the unit). ....

• Coin identification of penny, nickel, and dime
• Value of penny, nickel, and dime
• Counting a collection of pennies

• Skip counting by fives
• Counting a collection of nickels
• Counting on: adding a collection of pennies to a nickel

❑ Administer pretest. ....

To give sufficient time for correcting and compiling the information, administer the pretest a few days prior to the introduction of the unit.

❑ Compile results. ....

For example, if three students got the entire pretest correct, all students correctly answered questions related to coin identification, two students got all other questions incorrect (or didn't answer), and there was a smattering of other students who incorrectly answered particular pretest questions, the notes in my teacher's manual look as follows on my lesson introduction pages:
• Coin identification of penny, nickel, and dime (none)
• Value of penny, nickel, and dime (Sarah, Ali, Tommy, Katelyn)
• Counting a collection of pennies (Sarah, Ali)
• Skip counting by fives (Sarah, Ali, Anant, Tommy, Christopher)
• Counting a collection of nickels (Sarah, Ali, Anant, Tommy, Christopher, Heather)
• Adding a collection of pennies to a nickel (Sarah, Ali)

❑ Design whole group instruction. ....

Since all the children in the example correctly identified the coins on the pretest, I will combine the first two lessons of the unit into one whole group mini-lesson.

❑ **Prepare reteaching activities as necessary.** ....

> *The penciled-in names of students who got pretest question(s) incorrect helps me to remember to keep an extra eye on these students during my mini-lessons. I duplicate the necessary number of reteaching sheets for each corresponding lesson in the event that any student still appears to have trouble understanding the concept after the mini-lesson is taught and the guided practice is done. Such students will revisit the concepts during small group instruction. During small group instruction, students will use counters, sing songs that review skip counting, and use a hundreds chart to add money.*

❑ **Prepare enrichment activities as necessary.** ....

> *Students who correctly answered all questions on the pretest need enrichment activities. Since the example unit deals only with pennies, nickels, and dimes, these students will have an introduction, practice opportunities, and counting experiences with other coins: the quarter, half-dollar, and (if needed) the Sacajawea dollar. I also duplicate enrichment sheets for these students in case I need them.*

❑ **Design small group instruction.** ....

Lesson	Reteaching Activities	Enrichment Activities
Value of penny, nickel, dime	Use plastic coins to review and practice values.	Discuss value of a quarter and half-dollar.
Counting a collection of pennies	Show relationship between base ten ones blocks to pennies. Count collection of pennies.	Learning to give back change. Say, "The pencil costs 27¢. You have three dimes. What is the change?" Continue by saying the strategy: "Start with 27¢ and count on. 28¢, 29¢, and 30¢. The change is 3¢."
Skip counting by fives	Sing and dance to a skip-counting song. Turn over each numeral on a hundred chart when sung in the song.	Introduce skip counting of quarters.
Counting a collection of nickels	While singing a skip-counting song, count collection of plastic nickels.	Count collections of plastic quarters.
Adding a collection of pennies to a nickel	Use hundred chart to count a nickel with a collection of pennies.	Count a collection of pennies and nickels with a quarter.

❑ Choose
centers.

I always use centers that review previously taught content. I am also careful to select centers in a manner so that I am not collecting too many papers. Below are the center activities with the contents they review that I might use during a money unit.

Center	Activity	Skill
Computer	Grade-appropriate computer game	problem solving
Game	Try for 10	combinations of facts to 10
Listening	Bats Around the Clock	time to hour
Block	Tangram shapes	geometry, spatial relations
Graphing	Scholastic News blackline master	bar graphs
Number	Telephone Fun	multiple addends
Money	Let's Make Money	adding coins
Measurement	Measure the Room	standard linear measurement
Must Do	Problem of the day, Basic fact flashcard practice (last center)	problem solving

❑ Assess students with ongoing informal assessment during mini lessons, small group instruction, and center activities.

Assessment	Material	Evaluation
Ongoing formative	Spiral review sheets (a component of our math series)	Corrected; grades periodically assigned
Formal	District tests pertaining to content taught (various districts have designed standards-based assessments given to all children in a particular grade level)	Grade assigned
Informal	Beginning-of-unit pretest (return to students so they can correct all mistakes)	Not graded
Summative	End-of-unit test	Grade assigned

Math Learning Centers: Keys to Success

Grouping Students

Not to be confused with the flexible grouping that occurs for small group instruction, grouping in this context refers to the manner in which I place children so that they know which math and literacy center activities they must complete on any given day. This is a classroom management strategy I use unrelated to children's skill level.

At the beginning of the school year, I take my class roster and randomly divide the list into four groups. I balance each group with similar numbers of boys and girls while taking into account any needs individual students may have in order to create a heterogeneous grouping. Each group is assigned a color: red, yellow, green, or blue. As a visual aid, I have each child's name hanging in the classroom in the corresponding color assigned.

During the guided math block, children complete math centers according to their assigned color. On Monday, for example, the children in the yellow color group do the block center and the telling time center. The green group may have the money center and the addition center. As mentioned earlier, there are many parallels between my guided math and guided reading. Using the same color groups, children complete respective literacy centers during guided reading. On that same day, children in the yellow group may need to complete a word-making activity, use the computer, and complete a journal entry. The green group might use blocks to build their spelling words, continue writing a letter to a pen pal, and play a phonics game. As children participate in either their math centers or literacy activities, I am able to incorporate the small group instruction. As such, I may be calling up two children from the blue group, one each from the green and yellow, and none from the red group. Again, the color groups are established so that students know the center activities they will complete during the course of guided math (and guided reading), and the colors do not indicate the particular skill level of the students.

Tiering Centers—Making It Work for All Students

I am convinced that the learning center component of my guided math approach has given students a firmer grasp of the multitude of standards they have learned. I used to drive myself crazy by adapting centers to meet the needs of the "low," "average," and "high achieving" students. Very often this entailed entirely different materials for students to use. Now I provide tiered centers so that regardless of ability level, all students can use the same center. For example, using the ideas in Beach Ball Fun (page 21), let's assume the beach ball has a number (2–7) on each of the colored portions. A child tosses the ball in the air and catches it. She "reads her thumbs" to find that she has the digits 3 and 6. If she is still struggling with basic addition, she can show a one-to-one correspondence with the numbers or use counters to add the two numbers together. If she understands addition concepts, she can add the two numbers together and write the algorithm (3 + 6 = 9 and 6 + 3 = 9). If, instead, she is beyond basic

◆ Consider the grouping technique that best meets the needs of your students, taking into account the number of students in your class. If you like the idea of color grouping for students participating in center activities, you may need to incorporate additional colors. Ideally it is best to have no more than four to five students in a color group. You will get a better idea of the best way to group students as you continue to get a broader perspective of guided math.

◆ For more grouping suggestions, see *Great Grouping Strategies* by Ronit M. Wrubel (Scholastic, 2002).

addition, she can demonstrate repeated addition and/or a multiplication sentence ($6 + 6 + 6 = 18$ and $3 \times 6 = 18$ or $3 + 3 + 3 + 3 + 3 + 3 = 18$ and $6 \times 3 = 18$). As illustrated, all three practice opportunities use the same exact material. Your job, then, is to communicate the respective accommodation a child may need.

Developing Centers: Working Smarter, Not Harder

Developing center activities can be quite simple and I am continually amazed at the ease with which I have learned to integrate them into my teaching routine. Years ago, I used to labor over center development and I even tried to avoid it many times. My misguided notion was that centers had to be elaborate, with artistic activities displayed in an easily identified area of my classroom. When I had a class of 36 second graders, I quickly ran out of room (and ideas) and had to find better ways to accomplish this goal.

Although I want to provide a variety of centers, I do not want to increase the amount of paperwork I already have to manage. Likewise, in order to actually satisfy the students' mathematical needs, it is not necessary to spend inordinate amounts of time developing centers.

One way I use center activities is to provide experiences whereby children may review prior knowledge. One year, before my first-grade class began the unit on telling time to the half- and quarter-hour, I wanted to be sure that they could still tell time to the hour—a standard they should have learned in kindergarten. To help refresh their memories, I simply added a listening station activity to my centers. I have a book and corresponding tape called *Bats Around the Clock* (HarperCollins, 1999). In the book, time to the hour is reviewed in a whimsical and thrilling manner. As you can imagine, this was a very easy center to incorporate into my guided math block. At the same time, my reading in the content area standards came into play!

A "must do" center that all students in my class complete during our guided math block is Problem of the Day. There are many commercial versions for problem-solving activities. If your current math program does not include this component, you can try a supplemental book such as *5-Minute Math Problem of the Day for Young Learners* (Scholastic, 2001). My purpose for including it in our block is to better prepare the students for the high-stakes testing beginning in third grade. Most state tests require students to not only solve problems using algorithms but also to explain their answers in writing. Students in my class keep a Problem of the Day notebook, in which they respond to the daily posted problem—which also addresses the NCTM process standards.

Another center I incorporate consistently is a game center. Game play enables students to practice content and process skills, and also reinforces listening and speaking skills (both language arts standards). It is important for you, however, to choose games that provide practice opportunities in the content you want the children to review. There are many commercial games available. If you have a published math series, you may find several game opportunities in it. Do not make your game center a one-time experience. Allow students to revisit the same game several times throughout the year. As with all centers, be sure to communicate to students the standards they are practicing so that they, in turn, can communicate this with anyone who may come into your classroom.

Integrating Curriculum: Centers Right Before Your Eyes!

My primary source for getting center ideas has been in the teaching manuals I have in all the content areas. With the importance of curriculum integration, my reading, science, spelling, and handwriting manuals all suggest ways for me to incorporate math into the respective curriculum. In the past, I seldom used these ideas, as I had little time in that particular content area to accommodate them. But since implementing guided math, I have come to depend on many of these ideas. Likewise, I find it very natural to introduce the center to students during the content area from which the idea came.

For example, after reading *Animal Tracks* by Arthur Dorros as a shared reading activity, we discuss the many kinds of tracks made by animals. We also talk about the tracks that humans make. This leads to a brief overview of an upcoming guided math center to reinforce measurement with nonstandard units. I provide a short demonstration of the activity:

1. I trace my hand.
2. Next I make an estimate of how many sunflower seeds (a material available to me in my science kit) it will take to cover the outer edge of my hand.
3. Then I actually cover the edge with the seeds.
4. Together we count the seeds and determine the perimeter of my hand.

Using my hand gives children a frame of reference for when they will complete the activity. In turn, this center gives me a clearer understanding of their estimating and measurement abilities. Just as this idea is adapted from my reading manual's "Curriculum Integration" pages, you will find many great center activities from resources you already have.

> To keep all my center ideas organized, I use a three-ring binder with tab dividers. I put the name of the icon on the tab divider. I write the center ideas related to this icon directly on the divider sheet. I place any blackline masters behind the tab. If I have any teacher resource books pertaining to that center icon, I make a copy of the cover of the resource book and also place it behind the tab.

Managing Centers

The block of time in which you schedule guided math activities will determine the number of centers you are able to incorporate. However, I suggest that the last center available each day for all students, (regardless of their color group) is a basic facts practice. In my classroom, this takes the form of individualized flashcard sets. Children still trying to firm up addition to ten facts have a set that contains those facts. Those who are at the opposite end of the spectrum may have a set of multiplication cards for the tables 0–5. Flashcard sets may be bought commercially, be a part of a blackline master resource book, or be handmade by students as a center activity. In any case, students know that they continue to do this center until the guided math block comes to an end. This approach prevents them from rushing through centers to be the first one finished and exclaiming, "I'm done. What do I do now?" As I introduce the guided math procedure to children, I remind them that they are never finished. Basic fact practice is a very important foundation for many other math concepts. The more successful students are at mastering these facts, the more successful they will be in other areas of math. Occasionally, to provide a fresh approach, I introduce other ways for kids to practice these facts, such as adding number cubes or cards.

Using Learning Centers

You may recall from the chart on page 9 that center activities occur concurrently with small group instruction and independent practice. Therefore, as I continue small group instruction and the remaining students finish their independent practice activity, workbook page, or worksheet, children begin working with the activities in the math learning centers. Students interact with the centers that correspond with their color group. Again, learning center activities are key to the retention and maintenance of content knowledge. In the past, I had centers available that only reinforced the current content that we were studying. I have since realized that children need more practice with learned content in order to maintain their understanding. Thus, while teaching a unit on addition and subtraction with regrouping, one or two centers might address regrouping, but the other centers could address money concepts, calendar activities, telling time games, symmetrical art projects, and patterning challenges.

Many of the center activities provided in this book span two to four weeks. You will find these throughout, referred to as "ongoing centers." This simply means that total completion of an activity will take several separate visits to the center. For example, completing a class-made alphabet book relating to math could have a child arranging and gluing tangram shapes to make a letter of the alphabet during the first visit to the center. The second visit requires the child to write a corresponding sentence tying in that letter with a corresponding math word or concept. The third visit requires the child to illustrate the page. On the final visit, the child may enjoy reading the entire book assembled from all the classmates' pages.

At some point you will need to introduce each center to students. The more centers you can incorporate that are variations on a theme the less time you will spend discussing the use of the center. As indicated previously, I also make it a habit to incorporate tiered center activities. This allows many different students of varying math ability levels to use the same exact center materials. This strategy is outlined with many of the center ideas that follow.

Assigning Centers

You can use the centers with the various color groups on a rotating basis. For example, the green group may complete the telling time center on Monday. The blue group may do it on Tuesday, the red group on Wednesday, and so forth. I am not suggesting that the centers must be rotated each and every day. There may be a day during the week that you devote totally to whole group math instruction. I often do this with my problem-solving lessons. Therefore, during the course of that week, I may only have guided math on Monday, Tuesday, Thursday, and Friday. Another week my students go to the library, which does not give us enough time to have a guided math block on that particular day. Your rotation schedule and the number of days necessary for all students to get a chance to use a particular center will depend on many variables— especially the number of groups you set up in your classroom. If you have four color groups, you will need four guided math blocks in order for each student to have the opportunity to use the center, and so on.

As you first implement guided math, I recommend having just one center for the color groups to do during the math block. Your comfort level with the process will determine whether you incorporate a Problem of the Day activity or basic fact review. Keep in mind that it is important to reinforce proper procedures as you watch children participating in center activities.

When choosing the centers to use in the rotation, I am careful to blend the activities to monitor student practice in various ways. The monitoring may be done through my informal assessment, student interaction, individual monitoring, or through completion of the center itself. For example, I

As you can see in the chart below, on Day 1, one group uses the computer, another group plays a game, another completes a calendar activity, and the last group does a telling time review. Since only one of those activities requires paper and pencil, I end up collecting 4–6 sheets to check. As my guided math process has evolved, I have time to review these sheets during the guided math block.

Center Rotation

	Blue Group	Green Group	Red Group	Yellow Group
Day 1	Computer	Game	Calendar	Telling Time
Day 2	Telling Time	Computer	Game	Calendar
Day 3	Calendar	Telling Time	Computer	Game
Day 4	Game	Calendar	Telling Time	Computer

provide a reproducible for one center, math games for another, and create a self-checking center as well as a computer center. Again, I do not want to create a situation where I have a huge stack of papers to correct. Using the above example, I would only need to collect or check one set of papers. Since that color group has five children in it, I am only correcting five sheets. Keep in mind that you can use any time leftover after providing small group instruction to check these sheets. During this guided math block, I can also keep an eye and ear on the game center as the children play. I may ask students using the self-check center how they did. I can pull up a progress report for students using the computer.

In my classroom, I use icons to aid students in understanding their guided math responsibilities (see Appendix for reproducible icons). You may already use this type of charting system with guided reading activities, classroom jobs, or daily schedule. The medium you choose on which to display this might include a pocket chart, magnetic board, or bulletin board. I use clips and the surface of a closet door. Or you can simply write the name of the center on index cards and post them under a colored piece of paper representing the color group to complete the activity. To change the centers for the next guided math day, simply slide the center card or icon out of its clip and place it under the next color in the rotation.

When I am ready to add another color group center and/or the Problem of the Day and Basic Fact Review "must do" centers for children to complete at their desks, our classroom guided math door appears as it is pictured on page 19.

Managing Students

As you can imagine, there may be times during this guided math process where there is a potential for off-task behaviors or lack of understanding. To alleviate this, I give all students a "red light/green light."

Red Light/Green Light: This is simply one red and one green construction-paper circle glued back to back. I laminate them for durability. During the guided math block, all children display this tool on their desk or workspace. Green indicates that a student is progressing through the activity without difficulty. Red means he or she has encountered a problem of some sort. Although I instruct students to first consult a fellow color group member, if this does not help they must display the red light side but continue working through their color group activities. Even if a student docs not understand certain guided math activities, at the very least he or she is practicing basic facts (always the last activity of my guided math progression).

Between any small group or individualized sessions, I check for red lights and give the needed assistance. Playing soft instrumental music helps keep the noise level low. I also have a green, yellow, and red transparency circle displayed on my magnetic white board. I have a small magnetic disk for each child in my room. Each day all disks start at the "green" circle when guided math begins. If certain students are being too loud, or if they are off task, I ask them to move their magnets to yellow, a warning. If they get to red, they lose their privilege for guided math the following day.

Understanding the Tasks: Prior to starting the independent practice, we read the posted activities together so that all children understand their tasks. It generally takes less then one minute to do this, but it is time well spent. As an additional aid, I post the matching center icons in the place where children may need to get the materials. For example, if the red group uses the game center, I will have the game icon taped near the game they are to use.

For most centers, children within the color groups complete center activities independently, at their own pace. There are a few exceptions. For example, when I incorporate a game as one of the centers, I allow students within the color group to start the guided math process with that center rather than start with their independent practice sheet. That way the group may play as a whole. Generally I do limit the amount of time they may have to play the game (10 minutes) if it is one that cannot be completed in a short period of time. After all, the purpose of the game is to provide practice opportunities—not to establish a winner and a loser. Once students set up the game, one of the students sets a timer. You will need to decide what process is best for your group of children. After the game, children go back to their seat to start their independent practice sheet and continue down the list of activities posted. In another example, since only a few children may use the computers at a given time, those who are waiting continue with their guided math activities and use the computer once it is available.

Collecting and Correcting Finished Work: If a particular center has a record sheet or worksheet with it, you will need a collection procedure. I prefer to have all students keep the sheet at their desk until I ask for it.

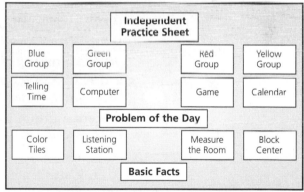

		Independent Practice Sheet			
Blue Group	Green Group			Red Group	Yellow Group
Telling Time	Computer			Game	Calendar
		Problem of the Day			
Color Tiles	Listening Station			Measure the Room	Block Center
		Basic Facts			

To determine what activities to do, students read the display from top to bottom.

Sometimes within the guided math block, I may call an entire color group up to discuss their answers with me. I can immediately assess their progress on the sheet and reteach as necessary (either within the time frame I have left in my guided math block or during my next guided math block.) Once collected and checked, all sheets go home. Remember to choose centers in a way that you are not collecting a record sheet from each of them on the same day!

It's a Privilege: I tell all students that guided math is a privilege. Once they get a taste of the process, they absolutely love all of its benefits. However, I let them know that any student who has persistent off-task behaviors or completes centers carelessly will lose this privilege the next day. If it is taken away (and there is at least one time each year that I must do this) I provide practice worksheets for the skill(s) the child would have reviewed during that next guided math block. Admittedly, it takes extra preparation and time for this, but in the long run, it is worth it. Once the other children see that the alternative to using guided math centers is completing a bunch of worksheets, they respect the materials, the activities, and the process of guided math and do their best to stay on task.

About the Centers

To help you implement the guided math approach, there are 35 learning centers on the pages that follow—arranged by NCTM content standards.

Many of the centers include variations, enabling you to provide the differentiation that is a key to meeting the diverse needs of your students. The reproducible sheets provide a record of the children's practice. Many reproducibles are generic so that you can use them with several skill levels and variation activities. Some masters may be more readily appropriate for your grade level, but all may be adapted easily.

Since the guided math centers enable you to provide the spiraling practice students need throughout the school year, you can reuse the same center materials with any of the variations listed (and children love to revisit familiar centers!). Additionally, "ongoing centers" require multiple visits to complete them. Remember, to avoid a lot of extra work for yourself, pick and choose those papers that you feel you must see in order to determine a child's success or lack thereof.

In the Appendix, you will find reproducible icons, student standards with parent involvement suggestions, and a substantial bibliography pertaining to each math topic covered in this book. The bibliography enables you to enhance your reading/book center and students' overall understanding of math concepts.

Beach Ball Fun

Materials

inflatable beach ball, permanent marker or adhesive numbers, record sheet (page 22)

Set Up

Place a number on each colored section of the beach ball.

Center Guidelines

Children toss the ball in the air. When they catch it, they "read their thumbs," using the numbers in the two panels where their thumbs are resting. Determine the number of times the children may toss the beach ball.

Activities

One-to-One Correspondence Using counting objects such as base ten blocks, beads, beans, or buttons, children count out the same number of objects that represent the numbers under each of their thumbs.

Whole Number Computation Children add the two numbers together or find the difference between the two. Provide counters for students who may struggle with this. More advanced students can multiply the two digits or demonstrate repeated addition.

Odd and Even Students identify their numbers as odd or even.

Place Value Students make all the digits possible by combining the numbers. Then they can put them in order from least to greatest. (Example: With a 2 and a 7, all possible numbers are 2, 7, 27, and 72.)

Number Sentences Children write number sentences using the two digits they read. (Example: 2 < 7)

Number Words Students write the corresponding number words.

Extensions

Algebra Children use all the numbers from three tosses to create a number pattern.

Geometry Children draw two shapes using their numbers, which determine the number of sides of each polygon. (This will only work for 3 or greater.)

Measurement Children find an object that comes between the measurements of the two digits (either with nonstandard or standard units).

Data Analysis and Probability Students use tallies to represent the digits.

Name _____ Date _____

Beach Ball Fun

First Toss:

Second Toss:

Third Toss:

Number and Operations, one-to-one correspondence

My Number Book

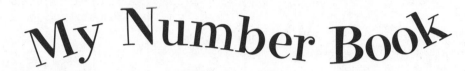

Materials
construction paper (two per student), lined drawing paper (ten per student), crayons, pencils, stapler

Set Up
Staple ten sheets of lined drawing paper (page 24) between two sheets of construction paper. Each child needs his or her own booklet.

Center Guidelines
This activity can replace any handwriting pages your students may use relating to the number words. This is an ongoing center, taking several sessions in order to complete.

Activities
During the first center session, students write a number word (in sequential order from one to ten) on each page inside the book. On their second visit to the center, students represent the quantities by drawing corresponding numbers of objects for each of the pages. The third visit gives children an opportunity to create a cover for their book. The final center session provides the opportunity for children to view other classmates' books. (Since my students visit this center once a week, this center ends up lasting for an entire month!)

Extensions

Geometry Students can illustrate their books using geometric figures.

Measurement Children can draw lines using the corresponding number to represent length in inches or centimeters.

Language Arts Students who are more able can write an entire sentence using the number word.

Social Studies Students who are more able can write words from other languages.

Telephone Fun

Materials

telephones, posted vocabulary words (from any
content area), calculators, record sheet (page 26)

Set Up

Display vocabulary or spelling words in some part of the classroom.

Center Guidelines

This is a great way for children to review vocabulary words or
spelling words. Demonstrate to students that each letter of the
alphabet is on a number pad of a phone. Using a word posted
in your classroom, demonstrate how the word's "value" can be
calculated. For example, the word "tree" would have the value of 21
by using the number sentence shown at right. Provide calculators
for those students who are not ready for multiple
addend addition or as a self-check feature.

$$8 + 7 + 3 + 3 = 21$$

$$t \quad r \quad e \quad e$$

Predetermine the number of words you expect
your children to total.

Activities

Using posted vocabulary and/or spelling words, children find a
predetermined number of words and calculate the words' values.

Extensions

Algebra Have students also write the number sentence that proves the value
of the word. Have them determine the word with the greatest and least value.

Geometry Use geometry-specific vocabulary. Have children use a 5 x 8 index
card. On one side write the word with its corresponding value. On the other
they draw a pictorial representation of that word.

Measurement Once the value is determined, have students show that number
in inches or centimeters on a yardstick or meter stick.

Data Analysis and Probability Have students graph the values of the
vocabulary words used.

Language Arts Have children use each word in a sentence.

Name _____ Date _____

Telephone Fun

My telephone number is ____ ____ ____–____ ____ ____–____ ____ ____ ____ .

When I add up all the digits the total is _____ .

Here are vocabulary words I know. I can add the value of their letters by looking on a telephone.

_____

When I add up the value of the letters the total is _____.

_____

When I add up the value of the letters the total is _____.

35 Independent Math Learning Centers Scholastic Teaching Resources

Hundred Chart Pictures

Materials

hundred chart (at least two per child), picture card, crayons, blank paper

Set Up

Using the picture card (page 28) and a hundred chart (page 30), make a sample for the students to view. Make additional picture card samples for your students that relate to various topics of study.

Center Guidelines

This is an ongoing center that lasts four rotations.

Activities

During the first center session, students create a picture using a picture card sample. On their second visit, students create their own pictures on a blank hundred chart. On the third visit, children write a corresponding picture card. The final center session gives children the opportunity to choose a class-mate's picture card to complete. You can bind these hundred chart pictures and picture cards into a class book for future use.

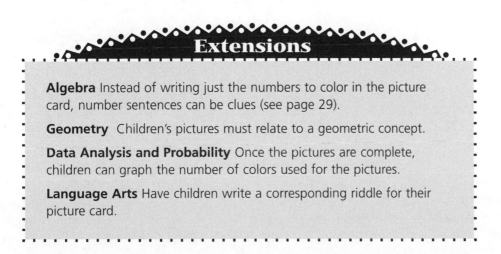

Name _____ Date _____

Hundred Chart

1	2	3	4	5	6	7	8	9	10
11	12	13	14	15	16	17	18	19	20
21	22	23	24	25	26	27	28	29	30
31	32	33	34	35	36	37	38	39	40
41	42	43	44	45	46	47	48	49	50
51	52	53	54	55	56	57	58	59	60
61	62	63	64	65	66	67	68	69	70
71	72	73	74	75	76	77	78	79	80
81	82	83	84	85	86	87	88	89	90
91	92	93	94	95	96	97	98	99	100

Extensions

Algebra Instead of writing just the numbers to color in the picture card, number sentences can be clues (see page 29).

Geometry Children's pictures must relate to a geometric concept.

Data Analysis and Probability Once the pictures are complete, children can graph the number of colors used for the pictures.

Language Arts Have children write a corresponding riddle for their picture card.

Picture Card

Riddle: I can grow tall. I can grow small. What am I?

Color these spaces on your hundred chart to find out!

GREEN:

5	6	14	15	16	17
24	25	26	27	33	34
35	36	37	38	43	44
45	46	47	48	52	53
54	55	56	57	58	59
62	63	64	65	66	67
68	69				

BROWN:

75	76	85	86	95	96

35 Independent Math Learning Centers Scholastic Teaching Resources

Name _____ Date _____

Picture Card Challenge

Riddle: I can grow tall. I can grow small. What am I?

Color these spaces on your hundred chart to find out!

GREEN:

7 − 2	3 + 3	7 + 7	20 − 5	8 + 8	18 − 1
12 + 12	30 − 5	13 + 13	28 − 1	11 + 22	36 − 2
20 + 15	18 + 18	40 − 3	36 + 2	45 − 2	22 + 22
50 − 5	40 + 6	49 − 2	24 + 24	55 − 3	50 + 3
60 − 6	20 + 35	57 − 1	52 + 5	61 − 3	57 + 2
65 − 3	3 + 60	32 + 32	70 − 5	40 + 26	69 − 2
18 + 50	80 − 11				

BROWN:

50 + 25	80 − 4	45 + 40	90 − 4	90 + 5	100 − 4

Name _____ Date _____

Hundred Chart

1	2	3	4	5	6	7	8	9	10
11	12	13	14	15	16	17	18	19	20
21	22	23	24	25	26	27	28	29	30
31	32	33	34	35	36	37	38	39	40
41	42	43	44	45	46	47	48	49	50
51	52	53	54	55	56	57	58	59	60
61	62	63	64	65	66	67	68	69	70
71	72	73	74	75	76	77	78	79	80
81	82	83	84	85	86	87	88	89	90
91	92	93	94	95	96	97	98	99	100

35 Independent Math Learning Centers Scholastic Teaching Resources

Try for 10

Materials
reproducible card deck (page 32), score sheet, pencil, counters

Set Up
Make 4 copies of page 32 and cut out the cards to create a deck.

Center Guidelines
This game is played with partners and should be demonstrated ahead of time.

Activities
To keep both partners engaged, have each keep score for his or her partner. Children who are still tentative with addition or subtraction may use counters.

Once children are comfortable playing this game, mix wild cards in with the numeral cards. When chosen, they may be used as any numeral!

How to Play Try for 10
1. Deal out four numeral cards to each player.
2. Use only two cards that, when added, give a total close to 10.
3. Write these numerals and their total on the score sheet.
4. Find your score by determining the difference between the total and the number 10.
5. Put the used cards in a discard pile. Keep the two cards not used for the next round.
6. For a new round, deal two new cards to each player. Make more numbers that come close to 10.
7. After five rounds, total your scores. The player with the lowest score wins!

Extensions

Kids who know regrouping concepts can play "Hurry to 100."

How to Play Hurry to 100
1. Deal out six numeral cards to each player.
2. Use only four cards to make two two-digit numbers. For example, 6 and 5 can make either 65 or 56. Try to make numbers that, when added, total close to 100.
3. Write these numerals and their total on the score sheet. For example: 81 + 23 = 104.
4. Find your score by determining the difference between the total and the number 100.
5. Put the used cards in a discard pile. Keep the two cards not used for the next round.
6. For a new round, deal four new cards to each player. Make more numbers that come close to 100. When you run out of cards, mix up the discard pile and use them again.
7. After five rounds, total your scores. The player with the lowest score wins!

0

1

2

3

4

5

6

7

8

9

10

Wild Card

Name _____ Date _____

Try for 10

Round	Cards	Difference
1	_____ + _____ = _____	_____
2	_____ + _____ = _____	_____
3	_____ + _____ = _____	_____
4	_____ + _____ = _____	_____
5	_____ + _____ = _____	_____

Total: _____

Name _____ Date _____

Hurry to 100

Round	Cards	Difference
1	___ ___ + ___ ___ = ___ ___	_____
2	___ ___ + ___ ___ = ___ ___	_____
3	___ ___ + ___ ___ = ___ ___	_____
4	___ ___ + ___ ___ = ___ ___	_____
5	___ ___ + ___ ___ = ___ ___	_____

Total: _____

35 Independent Math Learning Centers Scholastic Teaching Resources

☐ Try for 10 / ☐ Hurry to 100

Student's Name	Counts using whole numbers / Recognizes and writes numbers to 100	Uses concrete objects to count	Demonstrates understanding of one-to-one correspondence	Applies addition and subtraction using concrete objects	Determines if answer is reasonable	Makes, checks, and verifies predictions about the quantity of objects

Fish in a Boat

Materials

counters (reproducible icons, below, or fish-shaped crackers),
2 number cubes per playing group (of differing colors if possible),
boats (page 37), record sheet (pages 38–40)

Set Up

Copy the boats onto sturdy oaktag and laminate for a more
durable and reusable mat. Reproduce an appropriate record sheet
for students, as necessary.

Center Guidelines

Demonstrate the activity to the students.

Depending on
each child's ability,
the record sheet
may vary.

Activities

This activity may be done individually or with partners. If the
number cubes are different colors, students can determine which
one will represent the number of fish and which one will represent
the number of boats. If they are the same color, once the number
cubes are rolled, the students can determine which number
represents the number of boats and which represents the fish. For
example, if the numbers 2 and 4 appear, the two can represent
the number of fish to put in each of the four boats or the roll can
represent four fish put in each of the two boats. Either way, the
students are engaged in repeated addition practice. Once students
roll the number cubes they should put the corresponding number
of fish in the respective number of boats. Finally, they can figure
out the total number of fish.

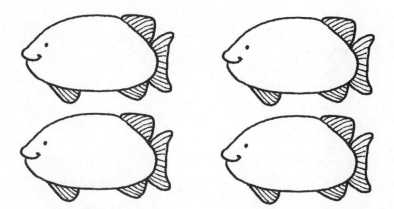

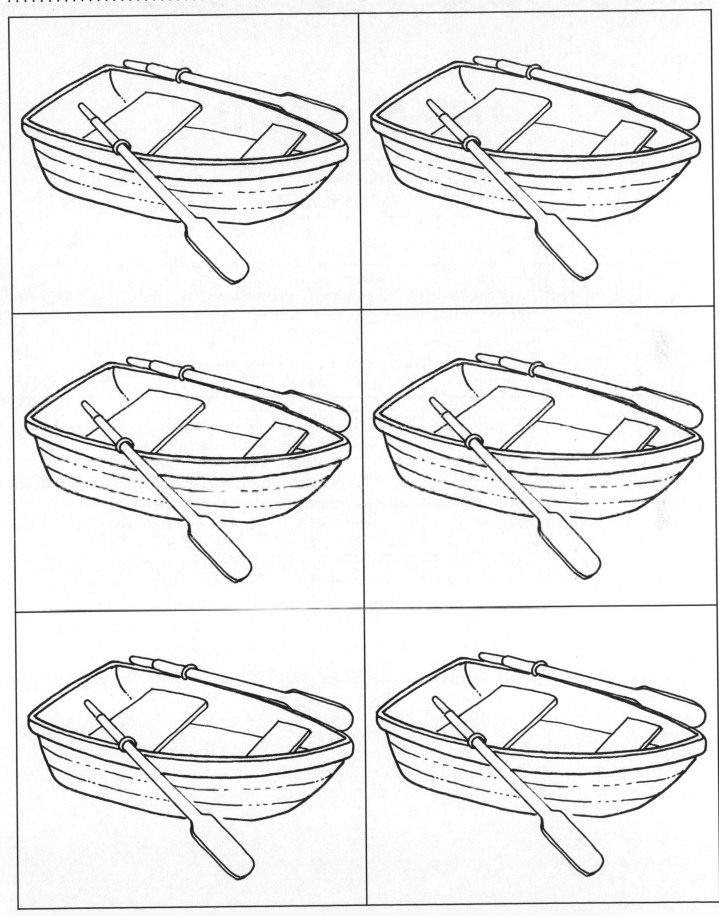

Name _____ Date _____

Fish in a Boat

Number of Boats	Number of Fish	Number of Fish in All
4	2	8

Here is how I play this game:

Fish in a Boat

Number of Boats	Number of Fish	Number Sentence	Number of Fish in All
4	2	2 + 2 + 2 + 2 =	8

Here is how I play this game:

Name _____ Date _____

Fish in a Boat Challenge

Number of Boats	Number of Fish	Multiplication Sentence	Number of Fish in All
4	2	4 x 2 =	8

Here is how I play this game:

Algebra, color patterns

Cereal Patterns

Materials
various colors of cereal rings, 3-oz. paper cups, record sheet (page 42), crayons, glue, pencil, gallon size plastic bags (optional)

Set Up
Pour cereal into cups.

Center Guidelines
Read the record sheet directions aloud.

Activities
Have students follow the directions on the record sheet. At the end of your guided math or center time, ask students to show their sheets to the class. Have members of the class name the patterns (AB, AABB, ABC, and so on). Before taking the sheet home, students may want to place it in a gallon bag to help avoid losing the cereal.

Extensions

Number and Operations Have students assign a number to the corresponding cereal colors to create a number pattern. More advanced students may want to make a pattern number sentence and figure out the sums.

Geometry Use cereal with different shapes.

Measurement Students can measure the lengths of the cereal patterns.

Data Analysis and Probability Children can graph or tally the total number of each color in a completed cereal pattern.

Name _____ Date _____

Cereal Patterns

Use two different colors of cereal to make a pattern. Use crayons to show your pattern.

Now try making a different pattern using three different colors. Draw your patterns using crayons.

Make a different pattern than above. Glue the cereal to show your pattern.

35 Independent Math Learning Centers Scholastic Teaching Resources

(**LEARNING GOALS**)

Algebra, color patterns

Pattern Bead Fun

Materials
various colors of beads, string

Set Up
Depending on the size of the beads (larger ones are needed for smaller hands), cut pieces of string long enough to accommodate 20 beads plus at least two extra inches.

Center Guidelines
Knot one end of the string for each student. Place various colored beads into sturdy containers to avoid spillage. Instruct students that the beads they choose need to represent a color pattern.

Activities
Have students make a pattern bead string by using a combination of 20 beads. Do not allow them to knot the other end until the pattern has been checked. Once constructed, allow classmates to name the pattern.

★TIP★

For younger or less-able students, decrease the number of beads.

Extensions

Number and Operations Have students keep these pattern bead strings in their desks to use as a counting aid when doing addition and subtraction. You can also use the Patterns sheet (page 44) for skip counting patterns. Students should continue each pattern and describe it.

Geometry Use beads with different shapes.

Measurement Students can measure the lengths of the pattern bead strings at various increments (for example, 5 beads, 10 beads, 15 beads, 20 beads).

Data Analysis and Probability Children can graph or tally the total number of each color in a completed pattern bead string.

Patterns

2, 4, 6, 8, _____ , _____ , _____

The pattern is _____ .

0, 1, 2, _____ , 4, 5, _____ , _____

The pattern is _____ .

22, 24, 26, 28, _____ , _____ , _____

The pattern is _____ .

30, _____ , 50, 60, _____ , 80, _____

The pattern is _____ .

30, 35, 40, _____ , 50, _____ , _____

The pattern is _____ .

120, 130, 140, _____ , _____ , _____

The pattern is _____ .

3, 5, 7, _____ , 11 , _____ , _____

The pattern is _____ .

35 Independent Math Learning Centers Scholastic Teaching Resources

Snake Stuff

Materials

color cubes (centimeter cubes, linking cubes, or color tiles), crayons, green 12" x 18" construction paper, glue, pencil, Snake Stuff (page 46)

Set Up

Reproduce one Snake Stuff sheet for each student.

Center Guidelines

This is an ongoing center. Have a completed sample available for students to view (see the directions on page 46).

Activities

During the first center session, students create a pattern using ten colored cubes. Then they represent this pattern on the very top of the Snake Stuff sheet using crayons.

On their second visit to the center, students color the snake to represent the color pattern they created on their first visit. The first color of their pattern should be colored on the snake's head.

On the third visit children cut out and glue the snake pieces together. Before the children glue the snake pieces to their green paper, suggest that they first arrange all the pieces. Then they should double check to make sure it represents the original pattern they created with the color cubes. Depending on your grade level or ability level of your students, this may be the final activity.

For others, during the fourth center session children extend the patterning concept to a number sentence. Using pencil, have children write the key for step 6 toward the top of the construction paper. The corresponding number sentence may be written toward the bottom of the sheet. The answer to the number sentence goes on the back of the paper. Once this part is checked by an adult and the information is correct, the student can trace over each with a thin, dark marker.

Assemble all the snakes into a class book. This book becomes a center in and of itself since the children can look at other students' snakes and figure out the answers to various numbers sentences.

Extensions

Measurement Students can measure the length of the snakes.

Data Analysis and Probability Children can graph or tally the total number of each color in a completed pattern.

Snake Stuff

1. Decide on a snake color pattern.
2. Color the snake consistently.
3. Cut out the pieces.
4. Assemble the snake pattern onto the construction paper.
5. Put your name on the paper.
6. Assign numbers to the colors in the pattern.
7. Use the numbers to make a number pattern.

Name _____ Date _____

Snake Stuff

An adult should read each of the statements below to the student while reviewing necessary terminology. Assign one point for each "yes" response.

	Yes	No	Comment	Points
I could recognize a color pattern.				
I made a color pattern using 10 cubes.				
I drew my color pattern on a sheet of paper.				
I described my color pattern to classmates.				
I copied my color pattern onto my snake parts.				
I gave a number to each color of my snake.				
I wrote a number pattern.				
I solved a number sentence pattern.				
Total Points	Overall Comment:			/8

Snake Stuff Kid Watching Sheet

Name of Child	Pattern recognition	Pattern description	Pattern extension	Pattern creation	Pattern replication

Break It!

Materials
10 linking cubes for each student

Set Up
Place linking cubes together in a group of ten to form a stick.

Center Guidelines
Demonstrate the game to all students. Although this center may be played individually, it is more exciting if children play in pairs or small groups.

Activities
Students place the linking stick behind their backs. One student at a time takes a turn to "break" the stick into two pieces. The student then shows one part to the other classmates. The other students try to decide how many links are still behind the student's back by using mental math or by using their own linking stick. Children take turns accordingly.

Extensions

Number and Operations Any number of linking cubes may be used depending on ability level of the students.

Measurement After breaking the stick into two parts, students can measure the length of each using standard or nonstandard units.

Data Analysis and Probability Once broken, children can represent the two parts using tally marks.

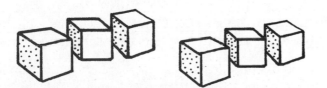

Open a Door 1 :: 0

Materials

9" x 12" light construction paper, colored adhesive dots (or any type of small sticker), markers, *Ten Black Dots* by Donald Crews (optional)

Set Up

Make several "door" templates (one per child) by folding in the two shorter sides of the construction paper to meet in the middle of the sheet. Place a number on the outside of one of these flaps. Open the "doors" and place the corresponding number of dots so that some dots are under the left flap and some are under the right flap.

Center Guidelines

If possible, introduce this center by reading *Ten Black Dots*. Use the door templates to play musical chairs by placing one on each chair. When children sit in their chair as the music stops, they must open one of the doors. Then they determine the number of dots hidden by the unopened door. For example, if the number 10 is on the outside of the doors and one opened door reveals 4 dots, the child should determine that there are 6 dots on the other side. After this introduction, tell students that they will be making their own doors.

Activities

Determine the number of doors each child may construct. Have a sample available for all to use. Depending on the age of students, you may want to prefold the templates. Children use markers and adhesive dots or stickers to create their own doors. (Kids may also color dots onto the paper using crayons or markers.)

Extensions

Number and Operations After making their doors, children can write the fact family that is represented by the numbers represented.

Measurement The number on the outside can represent the number of centimeters. The inside area can be a corresponding line. The students need to determine the number of centimeters left under the unopened door.

Domino Delight

Materials

set of double-sixes dominoes, paper,
pencil, *Domino Addition* by Lynette
Long (optional), record sheet (optional)

Set Up

Duplicate record sheet (page 52)
for each student, as necessary.

Center Guidelines

If possible, introduce this center by reading *Domino Addition*.
Using one domino, show the students the way that the domino
can illustrate a number sentence. For example: a domino with
four dots and two dots can be written as 4 + 2 or 2 + 4, both
totaling the sum of 6.

Activities

Predetermine the number of dominoes children should select.
Once selected, children show the commutative property for each
of the dominoes. To make this a game, children can play with
partners. Partners can select a domino from a pile of dominoes
placed facedown. The player with the highest sum wins. Play
continues for a predetermined number of picks from the pile.

Extensions

Number and Operations Students with accelerated ability may
play with double nines, double twelves or any other higher version
of dominoes. Also, students can write their number sentences both
horizontally and vertically.

Geometry Children can use the dominoes to create shapes.

Measurement After children find the sum of their dominoes, they
can draw lines measuring the corresponding number of inches or
centimeters.

Data Analysis and Probability Students can represent the sums
using tallies.

Name _____ Date _____

Domino Delight

First Pick:

Second Pick:

Third Pick:

Algebra, sorting and classifying

Button Bonanza

Materials

a variety of buttons, plastic-sectioned craft box, tackle box, or egg carton, record sheet (optional), crayons (optional)

Set Up

If you do not have access to the plastic-sectioned box, reproduce a record sheet (page 54) onto oaktag and laminate for durability.

Center Guidelines

Be careful about the number of buttons you place in the center. Too many may overwhelm the students. Children may work independently, with a partner, or in a group.

Activities

Students sort the buttons into categories. If desired, you may ask them to represent and describe their categories on the record sheet.

Extensions

Number and Operations Once sorted, children count the number of buttons in each section. More able students can add the total number of buttons sorted and represent this in a number sentence.

Geometry Once sorted, children can describe the shape of each button.

Measurement Once sorted, students can place the buttons from each of the sections buttons in a line. Each line can be measured to the closest inch or centimeter.

Data Analysis and Probability Children can graph the number of buttons in each section or graph the length of each line if they do the measurement activity from above.

Name _____   Date _____

Button Bonanza

35 Independent Math Learning Centers Scholastic Teaching Resources

Pattern Block Pictures

Materials

pattern blocks, pattern block templates (optional), paper, crayons, pencil

Set Up

Create a pattern picture sample or use the one below.

Center Guidelines

This is an ongoing center.

Activities

During the first center session, students manipulate the pattern blocks in a free-play manner. On their second visit to the center, students create their own pattern block picture and trace it onto a sheet of paper. On the third visit children color their pattern picture. Assemble all pattern pictures into a class book. The final center session gives children the opportunity to look at classmates' pattern pictures.

Students can discover beginning fraction concepts by using different blocks to recreate the pattern block picture.

Extensions

Number and Operations Students can count the total number of blocks or sides.

Algebra Students can assign a numeric value to each block and total the values of each picture.

Measurement Children can measure the approximate height and length of the picture.

Data Analysis and Probability Students can graph or tally the total number of blocks for each shape.

Language Arts Children can write a story to accompany their pictures.

Symmetry Trees

Materials

green construction paper, markers, crayons, scissors, miscellaneous art supplies

Set Up

Construct a sample for kids to see. Fold one sheet of construction paper in half. Cut out a tree (evergreen works well during the holiday season). Once opened, decorate one side of the tree with ornaments, apples, or any other decoration. Then decorate the other side as a mirror image of the first.

Center Guidelines

This is an ongoing center.

Activities

During the first center session, students create a symmetrical tree by using scissors and the fold of a green construction sheet. On their second visit to the center, students decorate one side of their tree with various art supplies. On the third visit children decorate the other side of their tree to match the first side they did. Ultimately, these trees may be used to decorate the classroom.

This activity is great not only for the December holidays but also for Arbor Day and Earth Day celebrations.

★TIP★

Rather than decorating the second side of their own tree on the third visit, students can trade trees and decorate a classmate's tree symmetrically.

Extensions

Number and Operations You may limit students to a specific number of decorations they may put on a side, thus reinforcing one-to-one correspondence.

Data Analysis and Probability Depending on the decorations used, children can graph or tally the items on the tree.

The Cat's Meow

Materials

tangram shapes, cat patterns, any cat-related book (optional)

Set Up

For durability, copy the cat patterns onto oaktag and laminate.

Center Guidelines

If possible, try to use this center after you have read a cat-related book. This may be an ongoing center if you use both cat shapes. In the Appendix of this book, you will also find other tangram shapes for students to use for future center visits.

Activities

During this center, students use spatial relations to arrange the seven tangram pieces to make the shape of a cat.

Depending on your students' familiarity with the puzzle shapes, you may want to give students the first cat with all the lines of the tangram shapes. On their next visit, with a different cat shape, remove a few of the lines leaving some from only one or two shapes. By their last visit, your students may be able to fill in the entire shape on their own.

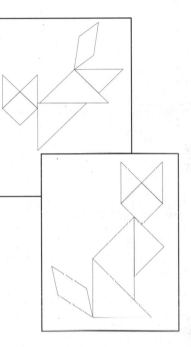

Extensions

Language Arts Read the book *Grandfather Tang's Story: A Tale Told With Tangrams* by Ann Tompert.

Matrix Solution

Number of Pieces	Triangle	Square	Rectangle	Parallelogram
1				
2				
3				
4				
5				
6				
7				

57

Tangram Matrix

Number of Pieces	Triangle	Square	Rectangle	Parallelogram
1			■	
2			■	
3				
4				
5	■	■		
6				
7				

Cat Pattern #1

Geometry, recognizing geometric shapes in the environment

Look Closely

Materials
record sheet (optional), paper, pencil, picture books (optional)

Set Up
Duplicate necessary number of record sheets (pages 62 or 63) if you choose to use them. Prepare a sample.

Center Guidelines
Be sure that your students have had experienced finding geometric shapes in real life objects before having them complete the record sheet.

Activities
Children look throughout the classroom (or use picture books) to identify geometric shapes in objects. If you plan to have the children use either record sheet, they will probably need a few visits to this center to complete it. They should write in appropriate objects under the corresponding shapes. You may also choose to adapt the record sheet or tell students during the center visit what their target shape is. For example, a teacher may say, "Today during the geometry center, those who visit the center will need to find three objects in our classroom that have a rectangle somewhere in its shape. Draw a picture of each on your paper using your pencil."

Extensions

Measurement After identifying the objects, students can measure the lengths of each using nonstandard or standard measurement.

Data Analysis and Probability Once the information is gathered from a group of children, they can tally the total number of objects representing each respective shape.

Look Closely

Circle

1. _____

2. _____

3. _____

Sphere

1. _____

2. _____

3. _____

Square

1. _____

2. _____

3. _____

Cube

1. _____

2. _____

3. _____

Rectangle

1. _____

2. _____

3. _____

Cylinder

1. _____

2. _____

3. _____

Triangle

1. _____

2. _____

Cone

1. _____

2. _____

Look Closely

Circle

Sphere

Square

Cube

Rectangle

Cylinder

Triangle

Cone

The ABC's of Math

Materials

construction paper tangram sets, 12" x 18" white construction paper, pencil, crayons, tangram letter and number sheet (page 65), glue

Set Up

Create a sample page for students to view.

Center Guidelines

This can be a very challenging activity for children. Be sure they have had a lot of experiences with tangram puzzles. If possible, enlarge the tangram letter sheet. This is an ongoing center.

Activities

For the first center session, assign each student an alphabet letter. Referring to the tangram letter sheet, students reproduce their respective letter on the 12" x 18" paper using the construction paper tangram set. Be sure that students orient their paper in the same direction for this project. Students should also place their letter towards the top left side of the sheet (leaving a bit of a margin to allow for the pages to be bound together into a classroom book). Children then glue their pieces onto the sheet. During the second visit, encourage students to think of a math term or idea that starts with their corresponding letter. Depending on your students' ability, they may either write this word below the tangram letter or write a sentence that includes this word. On the third visit, children draw a corresponding illustration for their page. Ultimately, bind these pages in alphabetical order into a class book. (You may need some volunteers to take an additional letter of the alphabet in order to complete your book.) The final center session gives children the opportunity to read the "ABC's of Math" book!

TIP

To create a tangram set, copy and cut apart any one of the tangram patterns in this book. Trace the outline of each piece onto construction paper. Cut out the seven pieces.

Extension

Language Arts The ABC book may be titled "The ABC's of Kindergarten," "The ABC's of First Grade," and so forth. It could be a culminating activity highlighting activities done in that respective school year.

The ABC's of Math
Tangram Letter and Number Sheet

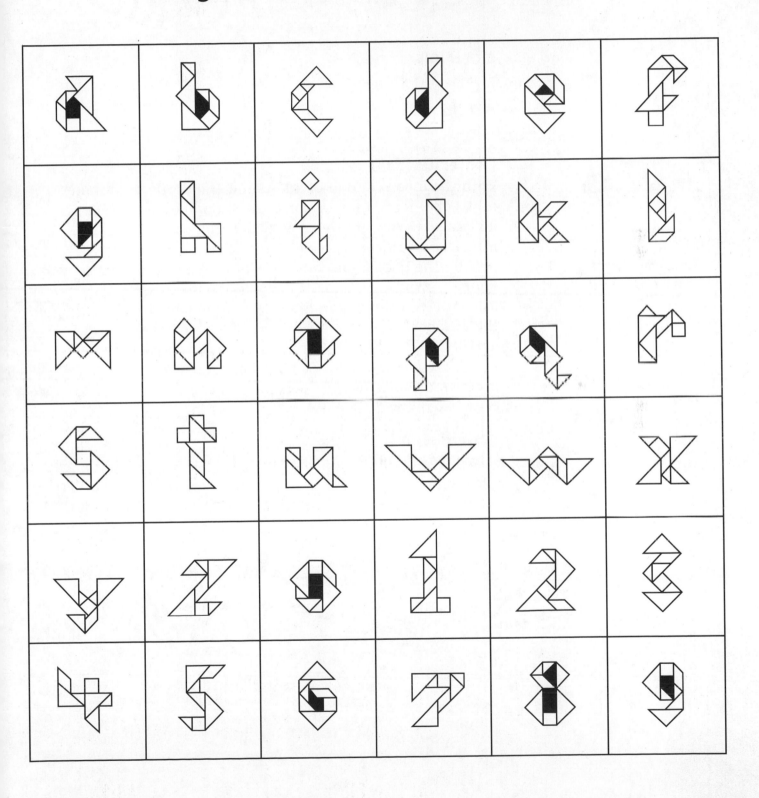

Seasonal Crafts

Materials
arts and crafts materials

Set Up
Always make a sample for students to view.

Center Guidelines
With the incorporation of additional standards, it is more difficult to have time for some traditional arts and crafts activities. Scrutinize these activities and see if you can integrate math concepts with any of them. Most activities require the use of objects that could reinforce geometric shapes, symmetry, and/or measurement concepts. Introduce the activity in a whole group setting, but allow the students to engage in the process as part of a center activity. Depending on the ability of your students, you may have pieces precut or have patterns available. Discuss troubleshooting ideas with the students prior to center activity.

Activities
These depend on the art activity selected.

TIP

If you have parent volunteers or a teacher aid, have them monitor this center activity.

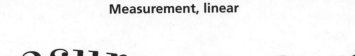

Measure the Room

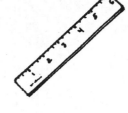

Materials
4 12-inch rulers, 4 infant or toddler size flip-flop sandals (available at a discount store), glue gun, record sheet (optional)

Set Up
Attach a flip flop to the 12-inch end of each ruler using hot glue. Having this sandal will not only serve as the pointer for the activity, but also it will help students remember that 12 inches equal 1 foot.

Center Guidelines
Demonstrate the center during whole group instruction.

Activities
This activity is the math version of "Reading the Room" that is popular with guided reading. Students use the ruler to point out objects in the room. Students may also use it to measure the objects. Decide whether you want children to use the record sheet. You also may want to change the intent for each center visit. For example, the first time they "Measure the Room," you might ask students to find three objects that are greater than one foot. The next time, they may find three objects less than one foot. Another time they may find objects greater than six inches but less than a foot, and so on. Children may record their answers on the accompanying record sheet (page 68) by either writing the name of the object or drawing a picture of it.

Extensions

Number and Operations Ask students to find objects using fractional terminology (such as one-half of a foot, one-fourth of a foot, three-quarters of a foot).

Geometry After measuring their objects, students determine the two- or three-dimensional shapes that they can find in the objects.

Data Analysis and Probability After measuring their objects, students put them in order from smallest to largest or largest to smallest.

Name _____ Date _____

Measure the Room

First Measurement:

Second Measurement:

Third Measurement:

35 Independent Math Learning Centers Scholastic Teaching Resources

Balancing Act

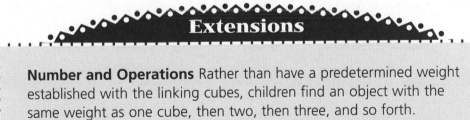

Materials
equal-arm balance, linking cubes, assorted objects, record sheet (optional)

Set Up
Be sure that the equal-arm balance is calibrated. Put assorted objects near the balance.

Center Guidelines
Demonstrate the center to all students prior to its use. Choose a predetermined number of linking cubes to represent the fixed weight for one of the balance bowls. Make sure that there are assorted objects that weigh more, less, and equal to the predetermined weight.

Activities
Children use the balance to find an object greater than the predetermined weight, less than the weight, and almost equal to the weight of the established number of cubes. Children may represent their findings using words or pictures on the record sheet (page 70).

Extensions

Number and Operations Rather than have a predetermined weight established with the linking cubes, children find an object with the same weight as one cube, then two, then three, and so forth.

Geometry Use attribute blocks or pattern blocks as the assorted objects. Children refer to the shape as they make their comparisons.

Data Analysis and Probability Students graph their findings on a chart or put the objects in order from least to greatest.

Name _____ Date _____

Balancing Act

_____ is greater than _____

_____ is less than _____

_____ is equal to _____

Cups, Pints, Quarts, 1/2 Gallons

Materials
large plastic storage container with lid, large bag of white rice, plastic measuring cup, pint and quart container, assorted smaller measuring cups (1/4, 1/3, 1/2, 3/4), record sheet (optional)

Set Up
Pour the rice into the large storage container. Place the assorted measuring containers inside.

Center Guidelines
It is imperative to demonstrate the proper use of this center. Provide ample opportunities for students to use this center in order to keep the concepts of volume fresh in their minds.

Activities
During the first center session, students freely play with the rice and various containers. As you observe students' interactions with this center, you will be able to gather a lot of information regarding their experiences with volume. On their second visit to the center, ask students to find relations among the containers within the storage bin. For example, you may ask students to determine how many scoops of the 1/4 cup container fit into the one cup container. Children continue with the 1/3 and 1/2 cup containers on subsequent visits. Use the record sheet (page 72) in the final center session so children can formally represent the relations between cups, pints, and quarts.

Extensions

Number and Operations Using a small spoon or scoop, children count the number of scoops needed to fill a predetermined number of containers. Once completed, the students add to find the sum of the scoops used and represent this using a number sentence.

Geometry Provide teaspoons and geometric nets for volume experimentation. If available, have students fill three-dimensional shapes (such as cylinders, cones, rectangular prisms, and so on).

Data Analysis and Probability Students can graph the results of their volume experimentation.

Name _____ Date _____

Cups, Pints, Quarts, ½ Gallons

How many cups of rice can you get into a pint? _____

How many cups of rice can you get into a quart? _____

Therefore, how many pints are in one quart? _____

How many quarts do you think are in a ½ gallon? _____

Therefore, how many pints are in a ½ gallon? _____

Draw a picture:

2 c. = 1 pt.   2 pts. = 1 qt.   2 qts. = 1/2 gal.

Animal Tracks

Materials

white construction paper, sunflower seeds (or some other object for nonstandard measurement comparison), pencil, record sheets (optional), *Animal Tracks* by Arthur Dorros (optional)

Set Up

Have a sample ready for students to view. Trace your hand onto a piece of white construction paper.

Center Guidelines

Demonstrate placing the sunflower seeds around the perimeter of the handprint. Then demonstrate placing the seeds inside the print (the area of the handprint). If needed, explain the directions on the record sheets (pages 74 and 75). If available, read *Animal Tracks* (Scholastic, 1991). Show the sample of your handprint to the students.

TIP

If the nonstandard measurement unit is consumable, students may glue it onto their handprint. If you decide to do this, a sturdier paper should be used.

Activities

During the first visit to this center, students trace their own handprint (or have classmates help by tracing each other's hand) and determine the number of sunflower seeds (or other item) it takes to fit around the outside (perimeter) of the print. The next time they visit, children determine the number of seeds to fill the inside (area) of the print.

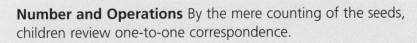

Extensions

Number and Operations By the mere counting of the seeds, children review one-to-one correspondence.

Geometry Students can trace geometric shapes and determine the perimeter and area of each.

Data Analysis and Probability Have students estimate the number of seeds they predict will cover the perimeter and area of their handprint.

Name _____ Date _____

Animal Tracks (Part 1)

1. Trace your hand onto the construction paper. Estimate how many seeds it will take to cover the outline of your hand.

   How did you determine your estimate?

_____

_____

_____

_____

2. Next, use the seeds to cover the outline. Write the number of actual seeds you used. Draw a picture of your handprint as it looks now.

3. The measurement around the outside of an object is called the

_____ _____ _____ _____ _____ _____ _____ _____ _____ _____ .

Name _____   Date _____

Animal Tracks (Part 2)

1. Look at the hand you traced onto construction paper. Now, estimate how many seeds will fit inside your handprint.

  How did you determine your estimate?

_____

_____

_____

2. Fill the inside of your handprint with the seeds. Write the actual number of seeds you used. Draw a picture of your handprint as it looks now.

3. The measurement inside of an object is called the

_____ _____ _____ _____ .

4. What observations do you think you would find if you did the same activity with your footprint?

The Race

Materials

record sheet (page 77), any version of *The Tortoise and the Hare*, cassette tape and player (optional)

Set Up

To turn this activity into a listening center, read the story onto a cassette tape.

Center Guidelines

Be certain that all kids know the story of *The Tortoise and the Hare*.

Activities

Children complete the record sheet individually or in a small group. They should compare the speeds of two objects, deciding which would be faster and which would be slower. Allow students to look in other books or areas of the classroom in order to get ideas to list on the sheet.

TIP

Children can draw pictures to represent slow and fast items rather than write the names of the objects.

Extension

Number and Operations Once they complete the record sheet, students can use the information to determine various attributes of the listed objects. For example, students can count the total number of legs, eyes, wheels, and so on, among the objects.

Name _____ Date _____

The Race

Faster

Slower

Example: hare

1. _____

2. _____

3. _____

4. _____

5. _____

6. _____

7. _____

8. _____

Example: tortoise

1. _____

2. _____

3. _____

4. _____

5. _____

6. _____

7. _____

8. _____

Time To...

Materials

clock sheet (page 79 or 80), white paper, crayons, *Time To . . .* by Bruce McMillan (HarperCollins, 1989), scissors, glue stick, construction paper

Set Up

In this activity, the children are making their own "Time To . . ." book based on activities in their life. Make a sample ahead of time so children have an idea of what you expect.

Center Guidelines

Read *Time To . . .* prior to students starting the center (or have the book available in the center). This is an ongoing center.

Activities

During the first center session, students cut out the clocks and glue each one onto a separate sheet of white paper. For the next two visits to the center, students may write a sentence that describes an activity that occurs at the designated times shown by the clock. On the fourth (and possibly fifth) visit children draw a corresponding picture for each page and clock in the book. The final center session enables children to create a cover using construction paper.

TIP

You can adapt the blank sheet on page 80 to meet your students' abilities.

Extensions

Geometry Children may use geometric shapes to illustrate the pictures of the book.

Language Arts Depending on the level of your students, you may want to incorporate an assessment appropriate for the writing aspect of the student-made book.

Time To . . .

Time To . . .

35 Independent Math Learning Centers Scholastic Teaching Resources

Name _____ Date _____

Time To . . .

An adult should read each of the statements below to the student while reviewing necessary terminology. Assign one point for each "yes" response.

	Yes	No	Comment	Points
I wrote the time for each clock.				
I started my sentences with a capital.				
I ended my sentences with a period.				
I capitalized the word "I".				
My title has capital letters for all the important words.				
I used my best handwriting.				
I used a reference to help me with my spelling.				
My drawings are neat and colored.				
Total Points	Overall Comment:			/8

Fishing Fun

Materials

red, yellow, pink, green, and blue linking cubes, small bucket, record sheet (page 83), pencil

Set Up

If you do not have linking cubes, cut out several red, yellow, pink, green, and blue construction-paper fish to place in the bucket. You may also wish to use the fish on page 36. Copy them onto colored paper, cut out, and and laminate for durability.

Center Guidelines

Display examples of tally marks in the center. Provide a different number of fish in each color. Instruct students not to look into the bucket when they pull out the fish.

Activities

Students go fishing by reaching into the bucket and grabbing a group of fish. Then they record their information using tallies on the record sheet. If they are using linking cubes, once they tally they can create a three-dimensional graph by connecting like colors together into bars.

★ Magnetic fishing sets are available at many dollar stores and can be used for this activity rather than the linking cubes. Students can use these to "fish" for five different fish and record the colors of those they "catch."

★ If you use construction paper, you can also make the fish magnetic by attaching a small piece of magnetic tape to each. Create a magnetic pole that students may use to catch the fish.

Extensions

Number and Operations Children can write a corresponding number sentence and a sum to indicate the total number of fish.

Measurement Once the linking bars are connected, students can measure their lengths.

Name _____   Date _____

Fishing Fun

Blue

```
[                                                          ]
```

Green

```
[                                                          ]
```

Pink

```
[                                                          ]
```

Red

```
[                                                          ]
```

Yellow

```
[                                                          ]
```

What does this chart show?

_____

_____

Our Favorite Colors

Materials
record sheet (page 85), pencil

Set Up
Create a sample record sheet.

Center Guidelines
This center should only be used after students have had several graphing experiences. Demonstrate the directions in a whole group setting.

Activities
During this center, students ask classmates to identify their favorite color choice. Children should write each classmate's name in the block that shows his or her favorite color. Then students color the graph.

Extensions

Number and Operations Students can create number sentences using the code of their graph. For example, using the graph below, blue plus red equals 8.

Geometry Instead of favorite colors, students can find out their classmates' favorite shape.

Measurement Using nonstandard or standard units, students can measure the length of the bars on the graph.

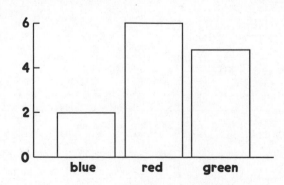

Name _____ Date _____

Our Favorite Colors

red	**yellow**	**green**	**blue**

What does this chart show?_____

_____

Name _____ Date _____

Our Favorite Colors

An adult should read each of the statements below to the student while reviewing necessary terminology. Assign one point for each "yes" response.

	Yes	No	Comment	Points
I surveyed everyone in my class.				
I displayed the data by coloring from the bottom up.				
I could tell an adult which color was chosen the most.				
I could tell an adult which color was chosen the least.				
I could tell an adult how many people in my class chose the color green.				
I could tell or show an adult the title of the graph.				
I could tell an adult how many people I surveyed altogether.				
I wrote something about my graph on the bottom of my sheet.				
Total Points	Overall Comment:			/8

Data Analysis and Probability, predicting likely and unlikely events

Let's Go Camping

Materials
record sheet (page 88), yellow crayon

Set Up
Duplicate a record sheet for each student.

Center Guidelines
In this center experience, students need to pretend that they are going camping with their family. Be sure to give them a lot of prior knowledge through classroom discussion or read alouds.

Activities
Students pretend to go on a camping trip. They should complete the record sheet by coloring in the face that represents their response. If needed, record the questions onto a cassette for the students.

Use other scenarios to reinforce children's ability to distinguish likely and unlikely events.

Extensions

Data Analysis and Probability Students can represent with tallies the number of smiling, sad, and neutral faces.

Language Arts Students can write their own statements and determine whether the event is likely or unlikely.

Name _____ Date _____

Let's Go Camping

	sure to happen	won't happen	may happen
1. I will see a bear.	☺	☹	😐
2. It will rain.	☺	☹	😐
3. A pink skunk will visit me.	☺	☹	😐
4. It will become night.	☺	☹	😐
5. I will see a rainbow.	☺	☹	😐
6. I will eat.	☺	☹	😐
7. It'll be sunny all weekend.	☺	☹	😐
8. I will see people.	☺	☹	😐
9. I'll go home on Tuesday.	☺	☹	😐
10. I will see Abe Lincoln.	☺	☹	😐

35 Independent Math Learning Centers Scholastic Teaching Resources

Data Analysis and Probability, creating a data sample

Penny Pitch

Materials
penny, record sheets (pages 90 and 91), pencil

Set Up
Duplicate record sheets for each student.

Center Guidelines
You may want to provide a piece of felt for the penny toss. Demonstrate the way children should circle "heads" or "tails" on the record sheet after each flip.

Activities
Students toss a penny 50 times and record their findings.

TIPS

✳ Try the same activity using a color spinner instead. If the spinner has four colors and they spin it a minimum of 50 times, children should be able to determine that each color has 25 percent chance of landing on it.

✳ Try the activity again using one number cube instead. For more advanced learners, once they have experience with the probability of one number cube, have them roll a set of number cubes. See if they are able to determine reasons why some rolls occur more than others.

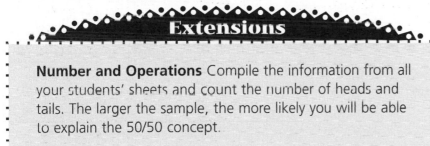

Extensions

Number and Operations Compile the information from all your students' sheets and count the number of heads and tails. The larger the sample, the more likely you will be able to explain the 50/50 concept.

Measurement Have children add up the total monetary value of the pennies that landed on "heads" and the total monetary value of pennies that landed on "tails."

Penny Pitch (Part 1)

1	H or T		26	H or T
2	H or T		27	H or T
3	H or T		28	H or T
4	H or T		29	H or T
5	H or T		30	H or T
6	H or T		31	H or T
7	H or T		32	H or T
8	H or T		33	H or T
9	H or T		34	H or T
10	H or T		35	H or T
11	H or T		36	H or T
12	H or T		37	H or T
13	H or T		38	H or T
14	H or T		39	H or T
15	H or T		40	H or T
16	H or T		41	H or T
17	H or T		42	H or T
18	H or T		43	H or T
19	H or T		44	H or T
20	H or T		45	H or T
21	H or T		46	H or T
22	H or T		47	H or T
23	H or T		48	H or T
24	H or T		49	H or T
25	H or T		50	H or T

35 Independent Math Learning Centers Scholastic Teaching Resources

Name _____ Date _____

 # Penny Pitch (Part 2)

Out of the 50 flips, how many heads did you get?

Out of the 50 flips, how many tails did you get?

Did heads or tails appear more?

What do you think would happen if you did the same activity with a dime?

Data Analysis and Probability, graphing

It's Lunch!

★TIPS★

* To make this more hands-on, use magnetic cookie sheets and have smaller versions of the same clip art pictures you use on your whiteboard. Children can then use magnetic numbers to indicate the total number of kids getting each type of lunch.

* With the magnetic cookie sheet, you can also use any type of clip art pictures that pertain to a content area your students are studying (such as animals). Students may then survey a certain number of classmates, asking them to identify their favorite (the number of choices will depend upon students' ability levels, but it's best not to exceed three or four). To represent the data, the children use the magnetic disks with their classmates' names on them.

Materials

magnetic whiteboard or surface, magnetic disks with each student's name (or initials), magnetic tape, paper, pencil

Set Up

Use clip art pictures to make a lunch sign appropriate for each of your school's lunch options (such as regular lunch, alternate lunch, packed lunch, and so on). You may want to laminate these for durability. Place these on your whiteboard along with the students' magnetic disks.

Center Guidelines

This is actually an effective procedure that can be used in your classroom. When children enter your classroom each morning, they need to move their disk to the respective lunch choice area.

Activities

During center time, students can graph (or tally) the number of children who are eating each type of lunch. If preferred, children may survey a predetermined number of students and represent the information using the whiteboard surface and magnets.

What Are My Numbers?

Materials
sticky notes, record sheet (page 94), pencil

Set Up
You will need to make a cover for the
class-made book that results from this center.

Center Guidelines
This is a great center to use after children have practiced
writing numbers during handwriting instruction. This
center lasts for two rotations.

Activities
Students each receive two sticky notes. Using their
neatest print, they write a number (ranging from 1–9) on
both notes. Next, they place the sticky notes on the back
of their record sheet. Then, they use those numbers to
calculate and fill in the answers to the questions on the
record sheet. (If appropriate, allow students to use
manipulatives to add or subtract the numbers.)

Once you have collected all the students' sheets and
have checked each sheet for accuracy, bind the book. If
necessary, you may want to add tape or glue to help
attach the sticky note answers more permanently. On
the students' second visit to the center, allow them to
read this self-checking book.

★TIP★

Revisit the center
towards the end of
the school year and
give the students a
higher range of
numbers from
which to choose.

Name _____

Date _____

What Are My Numbers?

When you add my numbers, you get

□

When you subtract my numbers, you get

□

What are my numbers?

Let's Make Money

Materials
Let's Make Money mini-book (pages 96–99), pencil, coin rubber stamps (optional), ink pads (optional)

Set Up
Make a sample mini-book.

Center Guidelines
This center was developed by a first-grade student (thus the author's name listed on the title page) but may be adapted to suit your students' needs. This is an ongoing center.

Activities
In this activity, children represent the coins using drawings or coin rubber stamps. Depending on the ability of your students, determine the number of pages to be illustrated during each center visit. The last page of the book requires the children to make their own monetary combination.

Extension

Number and Operations Children can make their own pages totaling an amount of their choosing and see how many different coin combinations they can make to equal that amount.

Let's Make Money Up to 20

written by Larissa Miller

illustrated by _____

Let's use 20 pennies.

1+1+1+1+1+1+1+1+1+1+1+1+1+1+1+1+1+1+1+1 = 20

I wonder what is next ...

Let's use 4 nickels.

$$5 + 5 + 5 + 5 = 20$$

I wonder what is next . . .

③

Let's use 2 dimes.

$$10 + 10 = 20$$

I wonder what is next . . .

④

Let's use 1 nickel and 15 pennies.

$$5 + 1 + 1 + 1 + 1 + 1 + 1 + 1 + 1 + 1 + 1 + 1 + 1 + 1 + 1 + 1 = 20$$

I wonder what is next...

Let's use 2 nickels and 1 dime.

$$5 + 5 + 10 = 20$$

I wonder what is next...

Let's use 2 nickels and 10 pennies.

$$5 + 5 + 1 + 1 + 1 + 1 + 1 + 1 + 1 + 1 + 1 + 1 = 20$$

I wonder what is next . . .

⑦

Let's use . . .

⑧

Using My Noodle

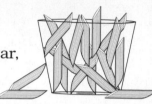

Materials

noodles (can be varying types and sizes depending upon the ability level of your children), large plastic jar, clear cups, pencil, record sheet (page 101)

Set Up

Pour noodles into the large plastic jar.

★TIP★

Reuse this center by adding smaller or different types of noodles.

Center Guidelines

Demonstrate this center as a whole group activity. Using a plastic cup, scoop noodles from the jar into the cup. Talk about the possible estimates for the number of noodles inside the cup. Discuss strategies. Place an estimate on the record sheet. Then count the actual number and record it on the sheet. This will help the students have a frame of reference when they go to the center for the first time. Finally, tell the children to represent the noodles by drawing them inside the cups on the record sheet provided and determine the difference between the estimate and actual number of noodles.

Activities

Students fill their plastic cup carefully with noodles. They estimate the total number of noodles and record it on their sheet. Then they count to find the actual number. Once completed, they draw noodles on the record sheet and find the difference between their estimate and the actual number of noodles.

Extensions

Number and Operations If different noodles were used, children can write a number sentence illustrating the different types of noodles scooped.

Algebra If different noodles were used, students can create a pattern using the various noodles found in their cup.

Geometry Children may use the noodles to create geometrical shapes.

Measurement Students can put matching noodles side by side and measure their lengths.

Name _____ Date _____

Using My Noodle

The number of noodles
I estimate to be in my
cup is _____ .

The number of noodles
in my cup is _____ .

The difference is _____ .

Making Numbers

Materials

pocket chart, index cards with numbers 0–9, record sheet (page 103), pencil

Set Up

Place a number on each index card (or use the reproducible numbers from page 32). You can adapt the record sheet to meet the needs of your students.

Center Guidelines

This is the math version of "Making Words."

Activities

Using the record sheet as a guide, students manipulate the numbers in the pocket chart to answer the questions.

Extension

Number and Operations Make additional Making Numbers sheets using the record sheet as a template.

Making Numbers

1 2 3

The lowest number I can make is _____ .

The greatest number I can make is _____ .

A two-digit number greater than 13 is _____ .

A two-digit number with a sum of three is _____ .

A two-digit number with a sum of five is _____ .

Mystery Number Clues

I have three digits.
I am greater than 200 but less than 300.
My tens digit is less than my ones digit.
What number am I?

The mystery number is ___ ___ ___

Number Sort

Materials
record sheet (page 105)

Set Up
If you plan to use the magnetic cookie sheets and numbers, have the numbers that the children are supposed to group listed somewhere.

Center Guidelines
This activity can be adapted depending on your students' abilities. There are several correct answers. When children complete the center, have them share their answers with classmates. Soon you will find that some children will try to find the most creative way to group the set of numbers. This center may be experienced over and over again using different numbers.

Activities
Students sort the set of numbers into two different categories. Then they write (or tell) why the numbers were grouped accordingly.

* For a more hands-on experience, students can group the numbers onto a magnetic cookie sheet with magnetic numbers.

* Rather than using the record sheet or the magnetic numbers, you could also use a pocket chart with index card numbers. Children can separate the numbers into two different areas and write each group's characteristics onto sentence strips placing the strips under the respective group.

Extension

Geometry Do the same type of activity using geometric shapes.

104

Name _____ Date _____

Number Sort

15   24   36   48   63   80   96   97

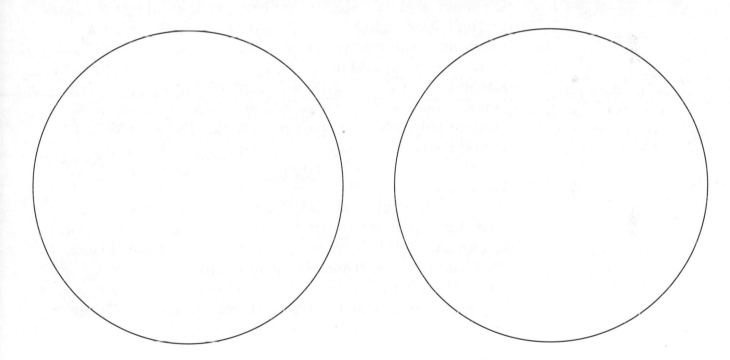

Reason:

Games

Materials
board games

Set Up
Prepare game materials as indicated by the instructions of the
respective game.

Center Guidelines
Commercial games are an excellent way to reinforce students'
math skills. In addition, it is a terrific way to build your
classroom community. Introduce each game in a whole group
setting. Play a round or two with some volunteers so that the
students actually see the game in play. One game can give
you an entire month of a guided math center. Since each
student only gets the opportunity to play the game once in
a guided math rotation, be sure to keep it as a center for a
longer period of time. Children are often eager to play the
game again.

Since most games require a minimum of two players,
allow any children who are assigned the game center to start
it immediately when guided math independent time begins.
Also, you must determine the game's duration. You may
choose to give a time limit allowing children to finish at recess
or you may even choose to have children complete the center
and forego a different guided math activity.

Activities
Students play the respective
game as instructed.

TIP

Using a sand timer
or other time-
keeping device is a
great way to let
children know when
their time is up at
this center.

Appendix

On the following pages you will find suggestions for involving parents in the classroom and learning process, along with an at-a-glance grid showing how the learning centers connect to the NCTM Standards 2000. Also included are various icons to help you organize your guided math block, supplemental tangram puzzles to help you extend learning, and an extensive list of book links for each math standard.

Parental Involvement

We need to involve parents and guardians in the education process as much as possible. Sometimes this is extremely difficult. However, the better the connection we have with students' home life, the easier our job can be.

The Giving Tree

Many times, our first contact with parents or guardians may be at a Back to School event. This is a terrific time to introduce your classroom's Giving Tree. The Giving Tree is an excellent way for parents to feel as though they are contributing to your classroom even though they may not be able to come into your classroom to volunteer their time.

   If possible, post the Giving Tree outside your classroom (for example, on a wall, whiteboard, bulletin board). Simply write items you would like to have on die-cut apples and hang them near the Giving Tree (see photo at right). Parents or other volunteers can find most of these items at discount stores. The following list includes items that pertain to centers found in this book.

- fish-shaped crackers
- metal cookie sheets
- magnetic numbers
- plastic cups
- noodles
- board games
- cereal
- telephones
- beach balls
- plastic measuring devices
- rice
- sunflower seeds
- ink pads
- coin rubber stamps
- 3 x 5 or 5 x 8 index cards
- buttons
- dominoes
- beads
- construction paper
- colored markers
- plastic resealable bags
- headphones
- cassette tapes
- cassette players
- kitchen timer
- number cubes
- spinners

Warm Fuzzies

We all like to get warm fuzzies. Incorporating these can really enhance your relationships with parents and guardians. On the next page you will find some samples to use. These notes, along with the appropriate food items, are a thoughtful and easy way to say "Thank you."

Miniature raisin box

Photocopy the note on the top of page 109 onto colored copy paper. Attach it to a box of raisins. Send this home to parents or guardians a week before fall conferences.

Microwave popcorn packet

Photocopy the note on the bottom of page 109 onto colored copy paper. Attach it to a packet of microwave popcorn.

Be creative! There are many foods out there that work well for this purpose.

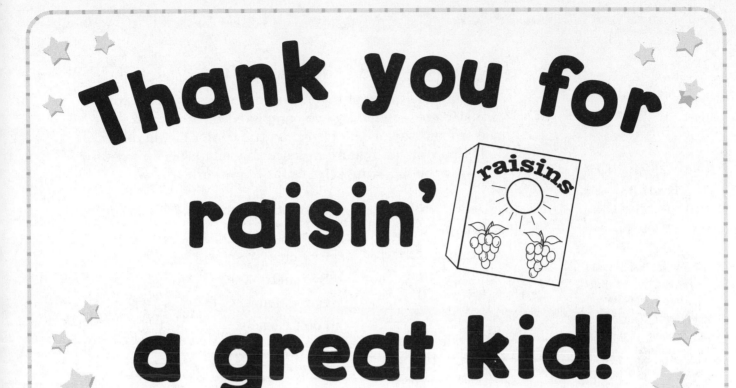

Thank you for raisin' a great kid!

Thank you for poppin' in to help us!

Our classroom is a lot of fun because of people like you!

Homework Fun

You may use many of the learning centers as homework reviews after students have completed the center in your classroom. Having children redo the center for homework helps parents and guardians see that math reviews can be fun. Try the following centers for homework review:

- Beach Ball Fun
- Telephone Fun
- Hundred Chart Pictures
- Try for 10
- Fish in a Boat
- Cereal Patterns
- Break It!

- Domino Delight
- Open a Door
- Button Bonanza
- Symmetry Tree
- Cat's Meow
- Look Closely!
- Measure the Room

- The Race
- Our Favorite Colors
- Let's Go Camping
- Penny Pitch
- Making Numbers
- Number Sort

Several centers culminate with a class-made book. Put the book inside a bookbag (or canvas tote) with a small notebook to create a "Traveling Book." Have children take turns sharing this traveling book with their families. Encourage both the student and parent or guardian to write a response to the book in the notebook. Then have the student share the response with the entire class. Centers that work well for this include the following:

- My Number Book
- Snake Stuff
- The ABC's of Math

- Time To . . .
- What Are My Numbers?
- Let's Make Money

You may also want to have a "Traveling Game." This works the same way as above. Because today's families are often so busy with evening activities, family game-nights seem to be a thing of the past. Encourage quality family time by sending home a classroom game that reinforces various math skills instead of a typical homework assignment. Allow students to keep the "Traveling Game" for a few days. Parents will be impressed with all the math concepts that are reinforced through the game!

Standards Connections

Please refer to the at-a-glance grid on page 111 for a quick way to see how the learning center activities correlate to the NCTM Standards 2000. While the grid shows how each main activity meets the standards, many of the extensions will help meet additional standards.

How Parents Can Help

The information on pages 112–120 includes suggestions of ways parents can help their children meet math standards. These ideas have been adapted from a document created at Dover Area School District, Pennsylvania, with the guidance of Sue Hoppe. Usually given to parents or guardians during the fall conference sessions, these suggestions detail ways children can experience various math concepts and meet math standards outside of the school setting.

Connections With the NCTM Standards 2000

	Number and Operations	Algebra	Geometry	Measurement	Data Analysis and Probability	Problem Solving	Communication	Reasoning and Proof	Connections	Representation
Beach Ball Fun	•				•	•	•	•	•	•
My Number Book	•					•	•	•	•	•
Telephone Fun	•	•				•	•	•	•	•
Hundred Chart Pictures	•					•	•	•	•	•
Try for 10	•	•				•	•	•	•	•
Fish in a Boat	•	•				•	•	•	•	•
Cereal Patterns		•				•	•	•	•	•
Pattern Bead Fun		•				•	•	•	•	•
Snake Stuff	•	•				•	•	•	•	•
Break It!	•	•				•	•	•		•
Open a Door	•	•				•	•	•	•	•
Domino Delight	•	•				•	•	•	•	•
Button Bonanza		•			•	•	•	•	•	•
Pattern Block Pictures			•			•	•	•	•	•
Symmetry Trees			•			•	•	•	•	•
The Cat's Meow			•			•	•	•	•	•
Look Closely			•			•	•	•	•	•
The ABC's of Math			•			•	•	•	•	•
Seasonal Crafts			•			•	•	•	•	•
Measure the Room				•	•	•	•	•	•	•
Balancing Act				•	•	•	•	•	•	•
Cups, Pints, Quarts, ½ Gallons				•	•	•	•	•	•	•
Animal Tracks				•	•	•	•	•	•	•
The Race				•	•	•	•	•	•	•
Time To . . .				•	•	•	•	•	•	•
Fishing Fun	•				•	•	•	•	•	•
Our Favorite Colors	•				•	•	•	•	•	•
Let's Go Camping					•	•	•	•	•	•
Penny Pitch	•				•	•	•	•	•	•
It's Lunch!					•	•	•	•	•	•
What Are My Numbers?	•	•			•	•	•	•	•	•
Let's Make Money	•			•		•	•	•	•	•
Using My Noodle	•				•	•	•	•	•	•
Making Numbers	•	•				•	•	•	•	•
Number Sort	•	•				•	•	•	•	•
Games	•	•	•	•	•	•	•	•	•	•

Kindergarten

The following information includes lists of the skills for each math standard your child should have, as well as ideas for helping him or her develop these skills.

Number and Operations

- Count to 30
- Identify and write numerals 0–20
- Use manipulatives to show a number (up to 20)
- Count groups of objects (up to 20)
- Show a number through drawings and symbols (up to 10)
- Show $1/2$ with drawings, diagrams, or models
- Count and identify pennies, nickels, and dimes
- Identify other coins as "not pennies"
- Compare numbers to 10
- Use manipulatives to count a group to 20
- Use manipulatives to order a group to 20
- Use manipulatives to group to 20
- Show how many (one-to-one correspondence)
- Estimate a group of objects in relation to 10
- Use manipulatives to show that addition creates a larger set/group
- Use manipulatives to show that subtraction creates a smaller set/group
- Orally state a reason for guesses and answers

Ideas

- Use newspapers to find various numbers from 0–20, cut out the numbers and glue them in order onto a large piece of paper. Ask your child to write down the numbers between those gathered from the newspaper.
- Make a statement that includes a number such as "I saw 17 birds fly by the window." Ask your child to write the numeral on a piece of paper.
- Include numbers in a statement such as "One boy and three girls are in the park." Have your child tell you how many children are in the park and show you the total with one red marble representing the boy and three green blocks representing the girls, for a total of four items.
- Have your child count to 10 using items such as beans, buttons, or rocks.

Algebra

- Use manipulatives to show an equation up to 5
- Use manipulatives to show the concepts of numbers to 20
- Use manipulatives to replicate an equal set (up to 5)
- Recognize, describe, extend, replicate, and create a pattern (AB, AABB, AAB, ABB. ABC)

Ideas

▲ Create simple patterns with sounds, movements, shapes, and colors and have your child continue the pattern. The sounds and movements can be generated by you and repeated by your child.

▲ Stamps and stamping pads are a fun way to make patterns with different shapes and/or colors.

▲ Children also enjoy starting a pattern and asking an adult to finish it.

Geometry

▪ Recognize and name a circle, square, rectangle, and triangle

▪ Build shapes with manipulatives

▪ Draw a circle, square, rectangle, and triangle

▪ Find and describe shapes in real life

Ideas

▪ Talk with your child about the different shapes that can be seen, cut, and colored so he or she becomes comfortable with the geometric shapes of circles, squares, triangles, and rectangles.

▪ Together, count the number of sides in a given shape.

Measurement

● Compare time (daytime/nighttime)

● Compare temperature (hotter/colder)

● Compare length (longer/shorter)

● Compare weight (heavier/lighter)

● Compare capacity (more/less)

● Compare time using authentic experiences

● Locate the classroom clock

● Identify numbers 1–12 on the clock

● Decide on a manipulative to use for measuring (thermometer/clock)

Ideas

● Make a clock using a paper plate. Put your child's first name on the short hand of the clock and last name on the long hand of the clock. Practice telling time to the hour by having your child read his or her first name (short hand), then last name (long hand).

● Model measurement-related language in conversation.

Data Analysis and Probability

▲ Given manipulatives, display data using pictures and a bar graph

▲ Answer questions about the data on bar graph and pictograph

▲ State a fact about the data on a bar graph and pictograph

▲ Using authentic experiences, understand how some events are more likely to occur than others

▲ Orally state a reason to support a prediction

Ideas

▲ Teach students to extend patterns and transfer them from one medium to another such as using a song with a pattern.

▲ Have your child create a graph with candy or cereal that has different colors and possibly different shapes that the family would be willing to eat later.

▲ Select any items that can be compared in terms of bigger or smaller; more, less, or equal; and higher or lower. Ask your child to indicate with examples for different family members such as "Which shoe is bigger or smaller?" or "Who has more or less milk in their drinking cup than I do?"

Process (Problem Solving; Communication; Reasoning and Proof; Connections; Representation)

▪ Identify numbers of a group based on similar attributes

▪ Use manipulatives to demonstrate and solve problems

▪ Explain how a problem was solved

Ideas

▪ Have your child experience with you counting situations like setting the table, selecting fruit at the grocery store, and picking out party favors for a celebration.

▪ Have your child experience with you how numbers are used for identification like room numbers at school, phone numbers, and house numbers of their friends.

Grade 1

The following information includes lists of the skills for each math standard your child should have, as well as ideas for helping him or her develop these skills.

Number and Operations

- Count to 100
- Count to 100 by 5's and 10's
- Count group of objects (to 100)
- Show/draw group of objects for numerals 1–100
- Write numeral to tell how many in group (to 100)
- Show $1/2$ of an object
- Identify pennies, nickels, dimes, and quarters
- Count groups of pennies, nickels, or dimes
- Count collections of pennies, nickels, and dimes
- Identify greater/lesser number to 100
- Put numbers to 20 in sequence
- Show how many (one-to-one correspondence)
- Show numbers to 100's (groups of tens/ones)
- Identify ones/tens place in two-digit numbers
- Estimate groups of objects (to 10)
- Demonstrate inverse relationship of addition and subtraction
- Add and subtract using concrete objects
- Solve addition and subtraction problems in horizontal/vertical form to 18
- Solve double-digit addition and subtraction problems without trading
- Estimate answers to 0, 10, or 100
- Determine if answer is reasonable

Ideas

- Share poems or songs like "Ten Little Monkeys Jumping on a Bed" and ask your child to count backwards with fingers or stuffed animals to represent the monkeys.
- Ask "how many" questions such as "How many chairs do we have?" or "How many doorknobs?" Then have your child count aloud, indicating the numerical value of each one found during the counting process.
- Using two decks of cards (remove the face cards), each person turns over one card and then your child tells if his or her card is more, less, or equal. He or she can also use the cards to learn about adding and subtracting. For example, your child can practice making statements such as 5 diamonds on my card + 2 hearts on your card = 7 diamonds and hearts altogether.
- Roll two number cubes and give their total value or the difference between the two.

Algebra

▲ Use concrete objects to model the concepts of numbers to 25

▲ Use concrete objects to model equations to 10

▲ Use symbols to model the concepts of numbers to 25

▲ Use symbols to model equations to 10

▲ Substitute a missing number in a number sequence

▲ Create a story to match given symbols and numbers

▲ Solve number sentences with manipulatives

▲ Explain solutions

▲ Explain meanings of symbols

▲ Recognize, describe, extend, replicate, and create a pattern

Ideas

▲ Using assorted colored cereal, have your child arrange the cereal into various patterns.

▲ Encourage your child to re-create the pattern on a sheet of paper using crayons or markers.

Geometry

▪ Name geometric shapes (circle, square, triangle, rectangle, and oval)

▪ Create shapes using manipulatives (circle, square, triangle, rectangle)

▪ Draw geometric shapes (circle, triangle, square, rectangle)

▪ Make rectangles, squares, and triangles on the geoboard

▪ Find/draw geometric shapes in real life

▪ Identify symmetry

▪ Combine or divide shapes to change them

Ideas

▪ Using geometric shapes, have your child create a colorful design.

▪ Go on a "Shape Hunt" around your home. Find as many circles as possible, and so on.

Measurement

● Compare length, weight, temperature, and time using words such as longer, shorter, hotter, colder, heavier, lighter, and equal

● Measure objects with nonstandard units

● Tell time to the hour and half-hour (digital and analog)

● Choose appropriate measurement tools

● Estimate and check measurements

● Measure several attributes of a single object

Ideas

● Using a variety of items, ask your child to compare length (shorter/longer), height (taller/shorter), weight (heavier/lighter), and temperature (hotter/colder).

To practice measuring with nonstandard units (a new pencil, a shoestring, or toothpick), select an object, such as a table, and ask your child to first estimate how many pencils long the table might be; then determine its length in pencils.

Data Analysis and Probability

▲ Gather, organize, and display data using pictures, tallies, charts, bar graphs, and pictographs

▲ Ask/answer questions based on graphs

▲ Form/justify opinion based on data

▲ State the likelihood of a chance event and explain reasoning using vocabulary such as "sure to happen," "sure not to happen," "might happen"

▲ List or graph possible result of an experiment

▲ Analyze data (largest, smallest, most often, and least often)

Ideas

▲ Select about 1 cup of various candy or cereal. On a piece of lined paper, have your child organize it into rows of similar color or shape.

▲ Have your child categorize various buttons.

▲ Provide your child with various plastic containers during bath time and talk together about the amounts that each holds.

Process (Problem Solving; Communication; Reasoning and Proof; Connections; Representation)

▨ Make and check predictions about quantity, size, and shape

▨ Use problem-solving strategies to tell a story, guess and check, and find a pattern

▨ Explain and justify the process used to arrive at a solution

▨ Use appropriate method and materials to solve problems using mental mathematics, paper/pencil, and concrete objects

Ideas

▨ Play a block-building game with your child.

▨ Read *Caps for Sale* by Esphyr Slobodkina with your child. Discuss the patterns seen in the cap illustrations.

Grade 2

The following information includes lists of the skills for each math standard your child should have, as well as ideas for helping him or her develop these skills.

Number and Operations

- Count to 1000
- Count to 1000 by 2's, 5's, and 10's
- Count groups of objects (to 100) using numbers
- Show the same number with concrete objects, drawing, word names, and symbols to 12
- Show fractions with drawing, diagrams, or models
- Count a collection of pennies, nickels, dimes, and quarters
- Compare collections of pennies, nickels, dimes, and quarters
- Identify even and odd numbers
- Identify greater/lesser numbers to 100
- Use concrete objects to count, order, and group
- Show and order numbers to 999 as groups of hundreds/tens/ones
- Identify ones/tens/hundreds place in three-digit numbers
- Estimate groups of objects to 100
- Round numbers to the nearest hundred
- Demonstrate inverse relationship of addition and subtraction
- Add and subtract using concrete objects
- Solve single-digit addition and subtraction problems in vertical form
- Solve double-digit addition and subtraction problems with trading in vertical form
- Use estimation to determine if an answer is reasonable

Ideas

- Use 10 paper cups or small containers that you label 1 through 10 and line up. Place a small item such as a button under one of the cups. Have your child try to find it by asking "Is the button under the fifth cup?" You indicate whether the button is before or after that position and your child continues guessing until the button is found. Beginning with five cups is a good idea until he or she understands the goal is to guess the object's location with the fewest number questions.
- Using any item that can be divided into two equal parts, have your child help separate the whole item into halves or fourths and then put the item back together to represent the whole. Sectioned candy bars and apples are easy to work with and also are a nice treat for working on math.
- Using only pennies, dimes, and one-dollar bills, you and your child take turns rolling a number cube to collect money with the goal that each of you must reach one dollar. After ten pennies are collected, they must be traded for one dime, and play continues until ten dimes are used in exchange for the one-dollar bill.
- Give your child a container and ask how many items (such as marbles) would fit. Have your child begin estimating a range of possibilities such as 20–40, and then actually fill the container, comparing the estimate to the actual result. Continue the process with the same container and different size items, and ask for the estimation ranges to narrow.

Algebra

- Use concrete objects to model the concepts of numbers to 50
- Use concrete objects to model equations to 18
- Use concrete objects and symbols to show an inequality

- ▲ Find the missing addend in number sentence
- ▲ Create a story to match a given symbol and number
- ▲ Use concrete objects and trial and error to solve a number sentence
- ▲ Explain a solution
- ▲ Recognize a pattern
- ▲ Change a pattern
- ▲ Gather information and display it in the form of a table or chart
- ▲ Describe and interpret data in tables and charts
- ▲ Describe simple function rules
- ▲ Locate points on a simple grid

Ideas
- ▲ Look around the neighborhood on the way to school and have your child find and describe patterns he or she sees.
- ▲ Discover patterns within your home.

Geometry
- ▤ Name geometric shapes in two and three dimensions (circle, sphere, square, cube, triangle, cone, rectangle, cylinder)
- ▤ Construct geometric shapes (circle, square, rectangle, triangle) using manipulatives and/or geoboards
- ▤ Draw and compare two-dimensional geometric shapes
- ▤ Construct rectangles, squares, and triangles on the geoboard
- ▤ Find/describe geometric shapes in real life
- ▤ Identify symmetry in geometric figures
- ▤ Identify symmetry in nature
- ▤ Discriminate between open and closed figures
- ▤ Predict how shapes can be changed by combining or dividing them

Ideas
- ▤ Look around your home with your child and note the geometric shapes found on walls, floors, ceilings, furniture, and fabric coverings.
- ▤ Find symmetrical patterns within your home.

Measurement
- ◉ Compare time, temperature, length, weight, and capacity using words such as longer, shorter, hotter, colder, heavier, lighter, and equal
- ◉ Measure objects with nonstandard units, U.S. customary units, and metric units
- ◉ Determine and compare elapsed time
- ◉ Tell time (analog and digital) to five-minute intervals
- ◉ Choose appropriate measurement tools
- ◉ Estimate and check measurement
- ◉ Measure different attributes of an object (length, weight, temperature, and capacity)

Ideas
- ◉ Using a variety of items, ask your child to compare length (shorter/longer), height (taller/shorter), weight (heavier/lighter), and temperature (hotter/colder).
- ◉ Using both digital and analog clocks, encourage your child to practice reading time by quarter-hour and five-minute intervals.

Data Analysis and Probability

▲ Gather, organize, and display data using charts, tallies, and pictographs

▲ Answer questions about the data on graphs

▲ Predict how many times something will occur based on data

▲ Form/justify opinion whether a given statement is reasonable based on a comparison of data

▲ Predict the likelihood of events and measure which event is more likely to happen

▲ List and graph the possible results of an experiment

▲ Analyze data using largest, smallest, most often, and least often

Ideas

▲ Ask your child to make comparisons of any candy or cereal you display, such as "There are more red candies than orange ones."

▲ Listen to your child's description of what he or she did to collect, organize, and talk about the displayed items.

Process (Problem Solving; Communication; Reasoning and Proof; Connections; Representation)

▦ Make, check, and verify prediction about quantity, size, and shape

▦ Verify and defend predictions related to real-life events

▦ Tell a story to solve a problem

▦ Guess and check to solve a problem

▦ Use a picture to solve a problem

▦ Make a list to solve a problem

▦ Find a pattern to solve a problem

▦ Make a table to solve a problem

▦ Use a five-point checklist to solve a problem

    1) understand the question   2) find the data   3) choose the operation/plan
    4) find the answer   5) check work

▦ Determine if sufficient information is given and explain how a problem was solved

▦ Use appropriate method, material, and strategy to solve a mental mathematics, paper/pencil, and concrete object problem

Ideas

▦ Order the license plate values and compare using greater than, less than and equal to your own family's vehicle.

▦ Put coins out on the table and have a discussion about what color and pictures are found on a penny, nickel, dime, quarter and discuss their value. Select a combination of coins with a value of less than one dollar and have the child count the coins to determine the total value.

35 Independent Math Learning Centers Scholastic Teaching Resources

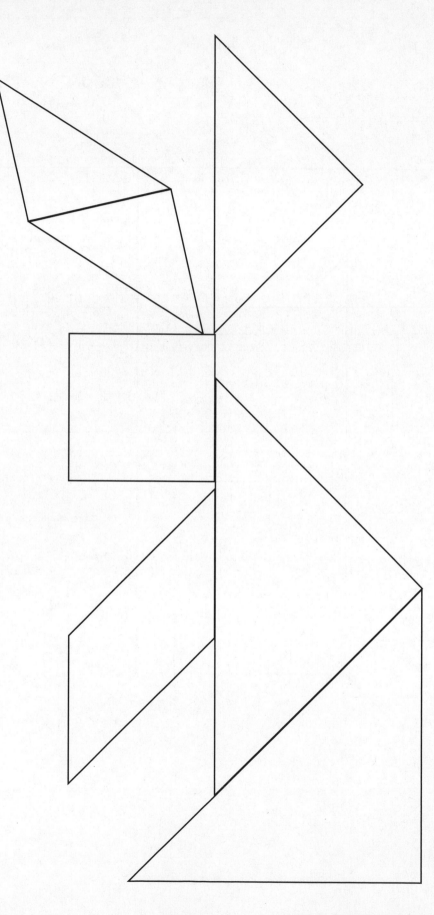

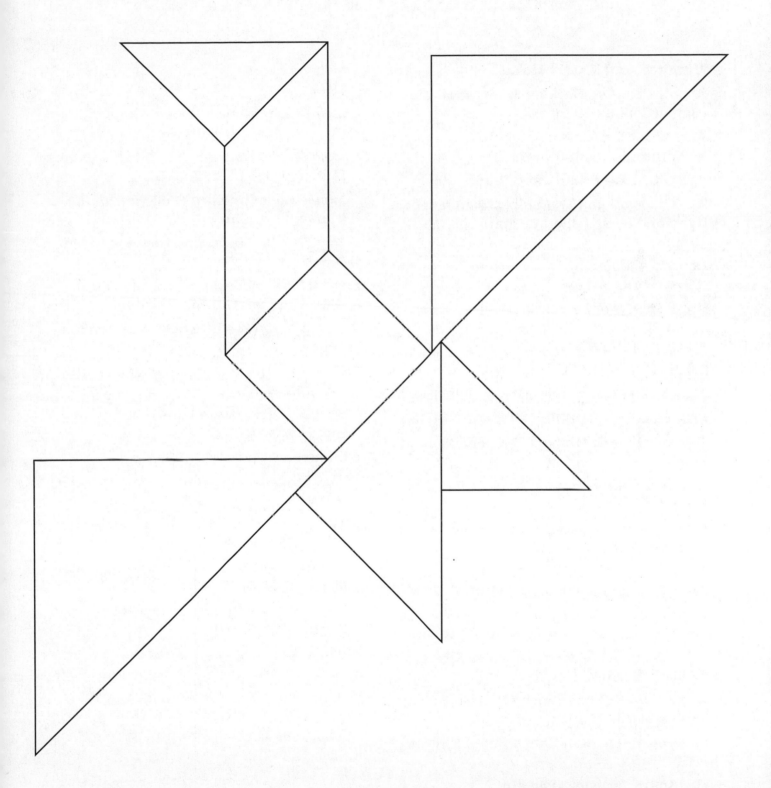

Additional Resources

Number and Operations

Anno's Counting Book by Mitsumasa Anno (HarperCollins, 1986)

Anno's Mysterious Multiplying Jar by Mitsumasa Anno (Putnam, 1999)

Apt. 3 by Ezra Jack Keats (Puffin, 1999)

The Crayon Counting Book by Pam Muñoz Ryan and Jerry Pallotta (Charlesbridge, 1996)

Domino Addition by Lynette Long (Charlesbridge, 1996)

Draw Me a Star by Eric Carle (Putnam, 1997)

Ed Emberley's Picture Pie by Ed Emberley (Little, Brown, 1984)

The Empty Pot by Demi (Henry Holt, 1996)

Fish Eyes by Lois Ehlert (Harcourt, 1992)

The Funny Little Woman by Arlene Mosel (Puffin, 1977)

Hattie and the Fox by Mem Fox (Simon & Schuster, 1992)

The Hershey's Kisses Addition Book by Jerry Pallotta (Scholastic, 2000)

The Hershey's Kisses Subtraction Book by Jerry Pallotta (Scholastic, 2002)

The Hershey's Milk Chocolate Multiplication Book by Jerry Pallotta (Scholastic, 2002)

How Much Is a Million? by David Schwartz (William Morrow, 1993)

The Hundred-Penny Box by Sharon B. Mathis (Puffin, 1986)

Imogene's Antlers by David Small (Crown, 1986)

The King's Commissioners by Aileen Friedman (Scholastic, 1995)

Millions of Cats by Wanda Gag (Putnam, 1977)

Moira's Birthday by Robert Munsch (Annick Press, 1988)

Moja Means One: Swahili Counting Book by Muriel Feelings (Puffin, 1976)

Mouse Count by Ellen Stoll Walsh (Harcourt, 1995)

One Fine Day by Nonny Hogrogian (Simon & Schuster, 1974)

One Hungry Monster by Susan Heyboer O'Keefe (Little, Brown, 2001)

1, 2, 3 to the Zoo by Eric Carle (Putnam, 1998)

Owl Moon by Jane Yolen (Philomel, 1987)

The Right Number of Elephants by Jeff Sheppard (HarperCollins, 1992)

Rooster's Off to See the World by Eric Carle (Simon & Schuster, 1999)

The Seven Chinese Brothers by Margaret Mahy (Scholastic, 1992)

17 Kings and 42 Elephants by Margaret Mahy (Dial Books, 1987)

Ten Black Dots by Donald Crews (William Morrow, 1995)

Two Ways to Count to Ten by Ruby Dee (Henry Holt, 1991)

What Comes in 2's, 3's, and 4's? by Suzanne Aker (Simon & Schuster, 1992)

When Sheep Cannot Sleep by Satoshi Kitamura (Farrar, Straus & Giroux, 1988)

Where the Sidewalk Ends by Shel Silverstein (HarperCollins, 1973)

The Wolf's Chicken Stew by Keiko Kasza (Putnam, 1996)

Algebra

Caps for Sale by Esphyr Slobodkina (HarperCollins, 1987)

Cherries and Cherry Pits by Vera B. Williams (William Morrow, 1991)

Cornrows by Camille Yarbrough (Putnam, 1997)

Curious George Rides a Bike by H. A. Rey (Houghton Mifflin, 1973)

The Important Book by Margaret Wise Brown (HarperCollins, 1990)

Jesse Bear, What Will You Wear? by Nancy White Carlstrom (Simon & Schuster, 1996)

Jump, Frog, Jump! by Robert Kalan (William Morrow, 1991)

Knots on a Counting Rope by Bill Martin Jr. and John Archambault (Henry Holt, 1987)

Rechenka's Eggs by Patricia Polacco (Putnam, 1996)

Geometry

Color Zoo by Lois Ehlert (HarperCollins, 1989)

Cubes, Cones, Cylinders, and Spheres by Tana Hoban (Greenwillow, 2000)

Geraldine's Blanket by Holly Keller (William Morrow, 1991)

Grandfather Tang's Story by Ann Tompert (Crown Publishers, 1991)

The Greedy Triangle by Marilyn Burns (Scholastic, 1995)

The Jolly Postman or Other People's Letters by Janet and Allan Ahlberg (Little, Brown, 2001)

The Most Wonderful Egg in the World by Helme Heine (Simon & Schuster, 1986)

The Paper Crane by Molly Bang (William Morrow, 1987)

The Quilt Story by Tony Johnston (Putnam, 1985)

Rosie's Walk by Pat Hutchins (Simon & Schuster, 1972)

Sam Johnson and the Blue Ribbon Quilt by Lisa Campbell Ernst (William Morrow, 1992)

The Secret Birthday Message by Eric Carle (HarperCollins, 1986)

Shapes by Tana Hoban (William Morrow, 1995)

So Many Circles, So Many Squares by Tana Hoban (William Morrow, 1998)

The Village of Round and Square Houses by Ann Grifalconi (Little, Brown, 1986)

Measurement

Alexander, Who Used to Be Rich Last Sunday by Judith Viorst (Simon & Schuster, 1980)

All in a Day by Mitsumasa Anno (Putnam, 1999)

The Carrot Seed by Ruth Krauss (HarperCollins, 1989)

A Chair for My Mother by Vera B. Williams (William Morrow, 1984)

Five Minutes' Peace by Jill Murphy (Putnam, 1999)

Giant Jam Sandwich by John Vernon Lord and Janet Burroway (Houghton Mifflin, 1987)

The Glorious Flight by Alice and Martin Provensen (Puffin Books, 1987)

The Grouchy Ladybug by Eric Carle (HarperCollins, 1986)

How Big is a Foot? by Rolf Myller (Dell, 1991)

Inch By Inch by Leo Lionni (William Morrow, 1994)

Jim and the Beanstalk by Raymond Briggs (Putnam, 1997)

Much Bigger Than Martin by Steven Kellogg (Puffin, 1978)

One Monday Morning by Uri Shulevitz (Farrar, Straus & Giroux, 2003)

Papa, Please Get the Moon for Me by Eric Carle (Simon & Schuster, 1991)

Patrick's Dinosaurs by Carol Carrick (Houghton Mifflin, 1985)

Pigs Will Be Pigs by Amy Axelrod (Simon & Schuster, 1997)

The Seasons of Arnold's Apple Tree by Gail Gibbons (Harcourt, 1991)

Strega Nona by Tomie dePaola (Simon & Schuster, 1979)

Sunday Morning by Judith Viorst (Simon & Schuster, 1978)

Ten Beads Tall by Pam Adams (Child's Play International, 1998)

Three Days on a River in a Red Canoe by Vera B. Williams (William Morrow, 1984)

Two Greedy Bears by Mirra Ginsburg (Sagebrush, 1998)

The Very Hungry Caterpillar by Eric Carle (Philomel, 1971)

Data Analysis and Probability

Cloudy With a Chance of Meatballs by Judi Barrett (Simon & Schuster, 1982)

Corduroy by Don Freeman (Puffin, 1972)

The Doorbell Rang by Pat Hutchins (William Morrow, 1986)

Hanukkah! by Roni Schotter (Little, Brown, 1993)

The Relatives Came by Cynthia Rylant (Simon & Schuster, 1993)

A Three Hat Day by Laura Geringer (HarperCollins, 1987)

Who Sank the Boat? by Pamela Allen (Putnam, 1996)

Problem Solving; Reasoning and Proof; Communication; Connections; and Representation

Anno's Hat Tricks by Mitsumasa Anno (Harcourt, 1993)

Across the Stream by Mirra Ginsburg (William Morrow, 1991)

A Cache of Jewels by Ruth Heller (Grosset & Dunlap, 1987)

Don't Forget the Bacon by Pat Hutchins (William Morrow, 1986)

Harriet's Halloween Candy by Nancy Carlson (Lerner, 2003)

The King's Chessboard by David Birch (Puffin, 1993)

Lon Po Po by Ed Young (Putnam, 1996)

Ming Lo Moves the Mountain by Arnold Lobel (William Morrow, 1993)

The Mitten by Jan Brett (Putnam, 1989)

Mr. Grumpy's Outing by John Burningham (Sagebrush, 1990)

1 Hunter by Pat Hutchins (William Morrow, 1996)

Q is for Duck by Mary Elting and Michael Folsom (Houghton Mifflin, 1980)

Teacher Resources

Cereal Math by Karol L. Yeatts (Scholastic, 2000)

Mega-Fun Card-Game Math by Karol L. Yeatts (Scholastic, 2000)

Shoe Box Math Learning Centers by Jacqueline Clarke (Scholastic, 2002)

Clifford® Number Set (Scholastic, 2004)